JESUS THE LORD

KARL HEIM

JESUS THE LORD

THE SOVEREIGN AUTHORITY
OF JESUS
AND GOD'S REVELATION IN CHRIST

Translated by
D. H. VAN DAALEN

OLIVER AND BOYD
EDINBURGH AND LONDON
1959

OLIVER AND BOYD LTD

Tweeddale Court
Edinburgh 1

39A Welbeck Street
London W.1

This is a translation of the fourth German edition of *Jesus der Herr: Die Herrschervollmacht Jesu und die Gottesoffenbarung in Christus*, published by Furche-Verlag, Hamburg, in 1955 as Bd. II of *Der evangelische Glaube und das Denken der Gegenwart: Grundzüge einer christlichen Lebensanschauung*, by Professor Karl Heim of Tübingen University.

The Scripture quotations in this book are from the Revised Standard Version of the Bible, copyright 1946 and 1952 by the Division of Christian Education, National Council of the Churches of Christ in the U.S.A., and used by permission.

ENGLISH EDITION
First published 1959

Translation © 1959, Oliver & Boyd Ltd
Printed for Oliver & Boyd Ltd in Great Britain
by Robert Cunningham & Sons Ltd
Alva

PREFACE TO THE FOURTH GERMAN EDITION

THE PRESENTATION of faith in Christ given in this second volume of *Christian Faith and Contemporary Thought* is meant for all those who today are moved by the question: is Jesus Christ merely a great personality of the past or is He the living Lord who can tell us with authority what we are to do about the burning questions of the present. This book therefore is not a dogmatic handbook in the sense of specialised theological discipline, but it endeavours to make clear the *either-or* with which the Lord Jesus confronts us and which consists in our either having to entrust our whole life to Him or passionately having to reject Him. That is to say: is Christ the One who lives forever, who has no need of our ability to vindicate Him because He himself is master of the battle and through all the centuries leads His cause to victory, entirely independent of whether we acknowledge or decline Him?

We are at present at the crossroads. Albert Einstein, who regards the development of the situation in the world with the cool objectivity of a great scientist and knows how fast the leading nations are developing the technical perfection of the hydrogen bomb, says that we have no idea how terribly little time we have left before the final decisions on the destiny of this our world will have been made. In this situation, in which the world hurries towards its final destination, we are extremely urgently confronted with the question whether the Man who once came forward with the stupendous claim that He was called by God to be the Consummator of our world's destiny, was right, or whether He was living in a religious illusion. As long as the historical development has not reached its end this question can be answered only in faith, and faith always means that individuals stake their whole lives, on this side as well as on the other side of the Iron Curtain, on this side as well as on the other side of continents and oceans. But this risk of faith is supported by the experience of a "cloud of witnesses" who have lived and died in this faith.

May this book, in its new edition, fulfil the task of strengthening men, especially those who have lived through terrible experiences and are living in fear of worse, in the certainty that our way as Christians has been placed between that which perishes and that which remains forever, "so that small things may be small to us and great things may look great" (*Dasz uns werde klein das Kleine | und das Grosze grosz erscheine*).

I would thank my friend Professor D. Otto Schmitz most cordially for having helped me substantially in preparing this new edition and completing it entirely in accordance with my wishes.

KARL HEIM

Tübingen, March 1955

CONTENTS

PART ONE

THE "UNKNOWN GOD", THE NEGATIVE CONDITION FOR AN UNDERSTANDING OF THE SOVEREIGN AUTHORITY OF CHRIST

1. The universal human need of a foundation of thought and action   3

    Secularism as the radical ungodliness: the question of our days that divides our minds.... Is belief in God inevitable for us men? .... The works of the law, and the Gospel as the two possibilities of positing a value.

2. The impossibility of satisfying the need of a foundation by our own effort   9

    The distinction between the two attitudes of trust.... Why does every authority carry the question of its legitimation within itself? .... What is polarity?.... Polarity and the state of indifference (Examples: rest - movement, colour - contrasting colour, sound - silence).... The original law of twofold polarity.... Polarity and the fundamental forms of our existence (space-time).... There is nothing anywhere that by itself is that which it is.

3. The reason why it is impossible for us to lay down a foundation of life   21

    The question of the "where" and "whence" of our existence.... Attempts to escape from the relativism of polarity by means of a position in thought.... The religious chaos of our times.... The meaning of *original* Being.... The insoluble contradiction between *original* Being and reality.... The solution of this contradiction.

4. The non-recognisability of God   28

    The two present possibilities of reaching knowledge concerning God: Spengler's and Juenger's views of the world.... In contrast, God as the Reality of all realities.... Hints as regards the recognisability of God in connexion with those two possibilities.... The only condition for a hearing of the Message concerning Christ.

PART TWO

THE SOVEREIGN AUTHORITY OF CHRIST

5. Self-guidance or guidance by Someone else   43

    The entirely unique element in the confession of the first Christians, "Jesus is Lord".... The inward attitude and the effect of allowing oneself to be led.... The values which determine self-guidance and some examples (rules of conduct, programme for the future).... Explanation of guidance by Christ as guidance by a living "Thou".

6. The early Christian confession "Jesus is Lord"   51

    Leadership in the biblical sense of the word can come from one
    authority only.... It demands a present "Thou" as Leader.... The
    meaning of the confession "Jesus is Lord".... Guidance by Christ,
    imagination or experienced reality?.... The decisive influence of
    guidance on the formation of a view of the world.

7. The element of truth in the Idealist belief in the possibility
   of self-guidance   64

    The offence of the Message concerning Christ begins with the
    demand that we should give up our self-determination.... German
    Idealism, especially Fichte, on the defence against this demand....
    The universally human element in this attitude of Fichte and the
    positive importance of German Idealism.

8. The breaking down of Idealism on Reality   69

    God-consciousness as part of our self-consciousness as contrasted
    with reality.... Results of God's mysteriousness: farness from the
    neighbour, the fate of Hamlet.... The reason for our need of ethics
    .... Other effects of our farness from God: indecision in action,
    weakness of will, lack of energy.... Suffering and the reason of
    suffering.... The experience of suffering (illustrated by Buddhism,
    Fichte and Luther) as an expression of farness from God.... The
    terror of death and the sedatives applied to it (materialism, the
    Indian return to Universal Life) as an expression of farness from
    God.... The reason for blindness to God is incomprehensible to
    him who is blind to God.

PART THREE

ORIGINAL SIN AS THE DEEPEST REASON WHY WE
NEED A LEADER

9. Satanic power in Jesus' view of the world   85

    Estrangement from God: fate or guilt?.... God as the original
    Reality and the Authority which needs no legitimation.... Our
    inability to answer the question of fate or guilt, therefore abandon-
    ment of the question of submission to the power of God.... The life
    of Jesus.... The struggle of Christ with God's mortal enemy and
    the latter's satanic defence.

10. The essence of the satanic   92

    Three statements on the essence of the demoniacal.... The rela-
    tion between the satanic will and our will.... The diabolical will:
    the will that wills in me and in all that lives.... Why men reject God.

11. The conflict between the Divine and the satanic   99

    The devil: an instrument of God.... The devil: a power that
    desires to dethrone God.

12. The two incompatible comprehensive views by which the belief
    in God lives   103

    Our farness from God is our own fault.... Our will of enmity
    against God, a superhuman, omnipresent will that desires to take
    God's place.... The dynamics of genuine faith in the contradiction
    between the sole agency of God and the attack on the reality of
    God.... "Faith" as distinguished from "vision".

13. Original sin and individual sin   111

 Can man be held responsible for something on which he has
never made a decision?.... Consciousness of guilt as an original
experience.... The guilt under which man lives before there is any
conscious deliberation.... Must the individual be the bearer of
guilt and responsibility?.... The reality of the diabolical power
present in all things.

14. Original sin and the form of the world   120

 Our state of being far from God in relation to the polar form of
existence of the empirical world.... The world: a sacred creation of
God's hand? Or: the mortal fate of the organic world.... a result
of our guilt?.... Separate development of those two views.... God's
"yes" to the polar form of existence of this world.

15. The contradiction between the two comprehensive views of
the world   129

 God's sole agency as one possibility for the form of the world....
The second possibility: the view of conflict.... The divine solution
of this contradiction.

PART FOUR

GOD'S REVELATION IN CHRIST

16. The incomprehensible fact   139

 Synopsis of the argument so far.... Is it possible that an absolute
leadership should be found in an altogether relative world?.... The
fact of the New Testament: there is an end to God's silence.

17. God has spoken   146

 The general statement: God's Message in the form of speaking
and hearing.... Speech as communication between man and man
.... God's Speech as explanation of God's silent display of power.

18. The contrast between God's Speech and God's silent Action   154

 The Message of God's Word is inaccessible to Nihilism and
Pantheism.... The Old Testament attitude to the Word of God....
The New Testament testimony on God's speech.... The Holy Ghost
as the ground which makes the encounter with the Word possible
.... The statement of God's speech leads to the Trinitarian formula.

19. God has spoken by the Son   163

 The content of God's Speech.... God speaks through a personal
"Thou".... Man's defence against God's Speech, particularly as
expressed by Hegel.... Listening to God's Word means giving up
one's own construction.... Autonomous choice of a leader means
self-guidance.

20. The Testimony of God's Revelation in Christ   169

 God speaks, not through an "it" but through a "Thou".... Hearing the words of a "Thou" as a commandment.... The contact
between Jesus as the Leader and the hearer of the Word.... The
aim of Jesus a contradiction of every aim of any other historical
personality.

21. Our contemporariness with Christ 177

Is personal discipleship of Jesus still possible today?.... The necessity of an "I-thou" relationship to Jesus.... The Pneuma as the lasting Medium of the "I-thou" relationship between God and mankind.... Christ: the Word of God itself.... Harmony between the present instructions of Jesus and the commandments of the historical Jesus.

22. The possibility and necessity of the Revelation in Christ to the present Generation 185

The fundamental view of the Old and the New Testament on the necessity of God's Word.... What was wrong about the belief in the god and father of Rationalism.... "He who sees me sees the Father"....Jesus is not someone of the past but One who is present and speaks right into the present situation.

PART ONE

THE "UNKNOWN GOD", THE NEGATIVE CONDITION FOR AN UNDERSTANDING OF THE SOVEREIGN AUTHORITY OF CHRIST

The Universal Human Need of a Foundation of Thought and Action

THE FIRST VOLUME of this work[1] brought home the question which is the ultimate issue in every philosophical discussion of the present time and also in ecclesiastical controversies. That is as yet not the question which started the denominational conflict in the days of the Reformation: *Wie bekomme ich einen gnädigen Gott*, how can I make sure of God's grace? The doctrinal controversy between the denominations which was once the cause of terrible wars has now very much receded. Neither is it the question that started a dispute among leading minds in the eighteenth century, e.g. on the occasion of the earthquake of Lisbon; the question whether there is a God who rules the world or whether its course is left to a blind fate. Earthquakes, volcanic eruptions, floods, mine accidents, famines which destroy hundreds of thousands of people, are things which the present generation takes for granted as something not at all out of the ordinary, and which does not call for any philosophical decision – especially since the atrocities of the second World War and the fear which hangs over mankind as a result of the development of the atomic bomb. The question which now divides our minds is more radical. It is the preliminary question which is to determine whether the whole controversy about religious matters and the intellectual work of theologians of all denominations has any serious sense at all, whether Luther's anxiety about God's grace and the eighteenth-century discussions on the demonstrability of His existence were not entirely without any object because it is *a priori* certain that the word "God" can never mean any more than a relative quantity belonging to this world, which men make the starting

[1] Karl Heim, *Glaube und Denken*, Berlin 1931; the third edition of 1934 is virtually a new book. Engl. transl. of the 3rd German edn. *God Transcendent* by E. F. Dickie, London 1935. Figures in brackets refer to the English edition.

point of their thoughts and actions. In the case of a sick man this is the repressed complex that dominates his actions from his subconscious; with a normal man it is some great cause which animates him, e.g. the honour of his tribe, or the knightly ideal of his ancestors, or the calling of the old business which he has inherited from his fathers. It is therefore always something that belongs to the empirical world. The mental attitude that is now spreading more and more is not the scepticism of the nineteenth century but a much deeper ungodliness, viz. what we now call secularism, the state of mind in which the question of God and His existence is no longer a question at all, but just the expression of a sentiment that irrevocably belongs to the past, and the problems of which to us modern men simply no longer have any object.

A man who has grown up in the old belief in God is inclined to think it unnecessary to enter into any discussion with this radical ungodliness. He says: there is no point at all in talking about God to people who have sunk so deeply: they lack the organ for it, one can feel sorry for them but we have to leave them to themselves. But according to what we said in the first volume we have to reply: we who believe in God are completely mistaken about our own situation if we think that the controversy with nihilism is merely a struggle with an enemy outside the walls of the Church and that we can leave the discussion with it to those who feel called to defend the foundations of the faith against these most radical adversaries. No, secularism is not merely an enemy outside the walls of the Church. We carry it within us. If we are honest with ourselves we have to admit that as often as anything comes between God and ourselves, so that we lapse from His fellowship, as often as we fall and against God's will get intoxicated with the world, God is not merely no longer a present reality but we have lost sight of the place where He was accessible to us. As the men of prayer in the Old Testament said: we shall first have to seek God's face again. The coherent system of this world, infinite in itself, in which there seems to be no room for God anywhere, which completely conceals the very thought of God, has encompassed us again and taken hold of us. Secularism, i.e. the radical ungodliness that has even lost sight of the question of God, is therefore a condition of the mind which we ourselves know only too well and into which we ourselves lapse again and again. Now, at a time when this mood is very noticeably in the air, this impresses itself much more forcibly on our minds than it did at times when belief in God was regarded as a matter of sound common sense. But however painful may be the discovery of this deep ungodliness which we not only see around us but which we also find within ourselves, the discovery has its advantages as well. This sorry state of affairs helps us to acquire a clearer knowledge of what is meant by the word God. Under the influence of Rationalism and Idealism the view has arisen that consciousness of God is a necessary aspect of our self-consciousness, that the thought of God is inevitable within the given world of our experience, that therefore irreligion can only be either self-delusion or dishonesty towards oneself. But when our eyes have been opened to our deep ungodliness, then we understand very well, it is true, how we arrived at that optimistic judgment of our situation, but we also see with alarming clarity that it was founded on a fatal confusion.

How did we arrive at the opinion that the idea of God is inevitable for us men? It rests on a fundamental fact that certainty does belong to our existence. Our existence, as Luther saw clearly, is not a state (*Ruhezustand*) but a *becoming* (*Werden*), a restless activity. In connexion with this it will be sufficient for us to quote some words of Luther's which Herbert Vossberg has collected in his work *Luthers Kritik aller Religion*.[2] Luther says that "human essence and nature cannot for a moment exist without acting or refraining from action, suffering or escaping (for as we see life never rests) . . .". Not only, therefore, must we make some kind of continuous physical movement as long as we live, but our spirit too is restless: "*Si igitur hominem voles vere definire, ex hoc loco definitionem sume, quod sit animal rationale habens cor fingens* (if you want truly to define man, then take the definition from this principle that he is a rational being with a heart that forms conceptions)."[3] Man therefore,

---

[2] Herbert Vossberg, *Luther's Kritik aller Religion*, Leipzig & Erlangen 1922.

[3] Vossberg, *op. cit.*, p. 39, Luther, *Sämtliche Werke*, edd. J. G. Plochmann and J. K. Irmischer, Erlangen 1826-57, VOL. II, p. 269. In references to the Erlangen edition of Luther's works, used by Vossberg, volume numbers in Arabic figures refer to German and in Roman figures to Latin works. Other editions quoted are the Weimar edition (*Kritische Gesammtausgabe*, ed. J. C. F. Knaake, 1883-) and the *Werke in Auswahl*, edd. Clemen *et al.*, 2nd edn. Berlin 1950-5 (cited as "Clemen").

according to Luther, has a *"ratio non otiosa sed semper aliquid fingens* (a reason which does not rest but is forever forming some conception)". But we can neither conceive nor think nor act without every moment making some ultimate assumption which we consider well-established. If we want to decide on an action we must regard as valid some value or some ultimate aim of life from which our action receives its sanction. If we want to think or calculate we must presuppose some logical and mathematical principles as fixed. In other words, we must always have some foundation on which to build our house. We cannot build anything without a foundation.

We can call the making of this assumption on which every theoretical or practical action rests "trust". For its validity no longer depends on proof. It is rather the foundation which must already be firm before any demonstration can be embarked on. But if we cannot prove the validity of something any further, and yet regard it as an established fact, build on it and reckon with it, then we can call this an act of trust. We then hold on to a support of which we cannot make sure in advance that it will not break. We set foot on a frozen surface without being able to make sure beforehand whether it will hold. The assumption therefore, from which we start, is an act of trust, no matter whether it concerns something concrete, e.g. our wealth, our physical strength, the progress of technical achievement, or something abstract, e.g. a moral or philosophical value or a mathematical axiom that serves as a starting point for our demonstration. As we saw, it is impossible to think, to live, to count or to act, and therefore to carry out any of those restless movements which according to Luther belong to our existence, without some assumption which itself cannot be proved. Consequently we can say that every living ego continually puts its trust in something. If we call this object of trust god, using the word god in its widest sense, then we can agree with Luther: "Man's heart must have a god, i.e. something from which he expects comfort, something in which he trusts so that it may rejoice and play."[4] Luther does not in the first place think of an abstract object, e.g. an idea or an axiom, but of material goods – money, wealth, physical strength – or of moral values, e.g. righteousness or wisdom. But whenever he speaks on the

[4] Vossberg, p. 40; Erlangen edn., VOL. 44, p. 203.

subject he adds an expression of completely indefinite generality: "*vel alia quaecunque* (or anything else)." That shows that he wants to include everything that at any place, at any time and in any sense could be an object of trust to someone. Therefore if with Luther we take the word god in this general sense we can say: "That, I say, to which your heart adheres, in which it trusts, actually is your god."[5] The necessity of building on something, trusting in something, regarding some presupposition as established we can, if we like, call a general religious disposition. But we must make no mistake: we then use the word "religious disposition" in such a general sense, that we obscure the serious *either-or* of which we become conscious when as responsible people we have to carry out such an act of trust in practical life.

As soon as I act in reliance on a value, I discover that there are two possibilities. Either I have to make and keep this value valid by my own act of confidence, or this value is there as the sustaining foundation of my trust, but entirely independent of any human trust. Luther expresses this contrast by saying: "That in which I trust is either God or an idol."[6] That in which I trust is either a self-chosen object of faith as according to Luther is the case with pagans – or I have found the ground which will hold my anchor forever, independent of my choice and action. According to Luther it can be said of all objects of reliance apart from revelation that men "actually make their own fictitious thoughts and dreams of God into an idol and put their trust in that which is nothing at all". It is only because of His self-disclosure that "God receives His honour that He alone is our strength, pride and joy, our florin and thaler, and that with all our heart we place all our confidence, pride and joy on Him alone. . . . This is duly honouring God and rendering to Him His glory and majesty: that one says: 'Dear Lord God, all that we have is thine, for we have not made it.' "

There are therefore two kinds of acts of trust, which can both be expressed in religious terms and which nevertheless have an opposite character. In the first case the object of trust receives and retains power and validity from the fact that there are many trusting people whose devotion sustains the object of

[5] Vossberg, p. 18; Erlangen edn., VOL. 21, p. 35; Clemen, VOL. IV, p. 4.
[6] Vossberg, p. 39; Erlangen edn., VOL. 36, p. 243.

B

their confidence. In the other case the existence and the value of the object of trust is independent of any human actions and states of the human soul. This object of trust therefore remains valid even when only a heap of ashes is left of the fire of our enthusiasm and devotion; it retains its glory even if we ourselves are no longer capable of any act of trust. In both cases we can speak of trust and yet in either case it bears a different mark. In the first case trust demands exertion, stamina, strength and ardour of the soul. People who live in this trust can be recognised by the pathos with which they speak about that which is most sacred to them, by the "deep tone of conviction" which betrays a more or less cramped state of their soul. On the other hand in the second case trust is an effortless repose, a being carried on eagle's wings, a being held by everlasting arms.

We could call the first kind of trust active because it exists only during the impetus of a great action. The second kind of trust we could call passive because in it we are ultimately merely passive and receiving. According to Luther active trust belongs to the works of the law, passive trust is possible only through the Gospel. It is part and parcel of our human existence that we have the ability to act and to make sacrifices not only if we have received this passive trust in which we are entirely relaxed and no longer in any cramped state. We can also live, suffer and die for a cause that does not support us but which we can only maintain in a state of ardent enthusiasm and active trust. In times of great success and victorious progress it is often hardly possible to distinguish between the two kinds of trust. Men of active trust and men of passive trust without distinction sacrifice their lives as a matter of course. But the contrast between the two kinds of men becomes fearfully manifest as soon as a reaction sets in and we are asked to make a seemingly senseless sacrifice for a cause that is humanly speaking hopeless, and to die unhonoured and forgotten at a lost advanced post. A trust which is possible only in the impetus of victorious hope collapses in this situation because it does not receive any nourishment. Only the man who has an ultimate obligation which supports him independently of his own efforts, can gladly make the sacrifice of his existence without any reward or success.

CHAPTER 2

The Impossibility of Satisfying the Need of a Foundation by Our Own Effort

FOR AN UNDERSTANDING of the biblical message concerning Christ it is essential that we should have a clear picture of the distinction between these two attitudes of trust. According to Luther the contrast between them determines the whole religious destiny of mankind. That is why we must attempt to examine this contrast till we get to its very roots. We therefore refer back to the detailed discussion of the subject in the final chapter of *God Transcendent*. There we made it clear where the dead point is, past which the secular attitude of mind cannot bring us, and what it consequently means, when the thought of God does get us past that dead point both in our reflexion and in our life. To this purpose we have separated the two central questions which again and again confront us in connexion with any theoretical knowledge and with every practical decision in life: the question "why?" in respect of the causal explanation of the world and the question "whence?" in respect of the ultimate sanction of our actions. It is quite sufficient if the dead point which we cannot pass by our own strength has been made clear in respect of these two fundamental conditions of our existence. We then know immediately that we are faced with a law of existence which lends their common character to all relations in which we live and think.

We have seen that the question "why?" and the question "whence?" in respect of authority cannot be silenced. For every *"original* state"[1] which serves as the initial point of an explanation of the world, and every final authority from which the legitimacy of our action is derived always contain the question: but why should this be the *original* state? Whence has the final authority its authority? In both cases there is no end to it. One might perhaps think that this is due to the par-

[1] Cf. p. 23, note 2.

ticular structure of the principle of causality or to the way in which the authority is sanctioned. But simple reflexion will show that the contrast with which we are here confronted applies to all relations in which we are placed. In whatever relation we may move, we always make a movement which we cannot cut short and stop. Each time we go through a series of which we cannot reach the end. Anything that we measure, no matter whether it is the length of a street or the content of a liquid or the weight of a metal or the temperature of a room, we always measure by some measure. But this must be measured by another measure, and so on. Of course, in this process of measuring one quantity by another we have to stop somewhere. We must acknowledge some instrument for measuring as a standard, an *original* measure which we no longer measure by anything else but which we treat as a fixed quantity. But we know that in doing this we have arbitrarily stopped at a certain point. In the same way every logical and mathematical demonstration depends on axioms which cannot themselves be proved but which are regarded as "self-evident" and serve as a basis for all further demonstration. We realise that we have to take the validity of these axioms for granted because no demonstration would be possible without them. But this cannot silence the question concerning the legitimacy or the validity of these presuppositions and measures. This question remains alive and drives us to continual efforts to get behind these axioms by means of our reflexion. Anselm, for whose demonstration of the existence of God this fact was rather awkward, endeavoured to do away with it by simply declaring that anyone who maintained that there is no end to the series in which we are led back from one link to the other, is mad. He says: "*Si enim huiusmodi graduum distinctio sic est infinita, ut nullus ibi sit gradus superior, quo superior alius non invenitur, ad hoc ratio deducitur, ut ipsarum multitudo naturarum nullo fine claudatur. Hoc autem nemo non putat absurdum, nisi qui nimis est absurdus* (For if such a distinction of degrees is so infinite, that there is no higher degree without our finding another degree which is higher yet, then our reason must conclude that there is no end to the number of natures. But only he who is mad himself can avoid regarding this idea as mad)."[2]

---

[2] Cf. Ernst Haenchen, "Wort und Geist", in *Festgabe für Karl Heim*, edd. A. Köberle and O. Schmitz, Berlin 1934, p. 189.

Schlatter declares to the same effect: "Or do we perhaps find an infinite series and do we for every cause need another cause, for God another God to create him etc. *ad infinitum*? This thought would be the product of a fanatic 'pure' reason which would endeavour to think without using experience."[3] It is possible to give such an opinion. But even so no one, not even Anselm and Schlatter, can conceive any final cause as the end of a chain or as the basis of a demonstration, without immediately being faced with the question: whence comes that final cause? Why is that ultimate basis valid? We can crush the question the moment it arises, by calling it madness or fanaticism. Nevertheless the question is there. It was already asked before we silenced it in this arbitrary manner. We cannot escape the question, even though we try to send it to a lunatic asylum, so that we need not enter into any discussion with it, because we find it awkward. If we are not prepared to admit this, then *we* are the "fanatics". Then we disregard the fundamental law of perception and conception, which prohibits us once and for all to conceive the initial link of such a chain.

Why is it that this question is inevitable and inescapable? Why does every cause from which we try to explain the world point with necessity to another further cause? Why does every authority carry with it the question as to its legitimacy? Why does every measure by which we measure something, presuppose another measure by which it is itself measured? Why in all these cases is the reflexion irresistibly made to go further? We cannot explain this, but we can reduce the fact which here confronts us to a universal law, applicable to the whole structure of the world of I-thou-it in which we have been placed. That is the law of polarity which is the basis of all distinctions which we have to make within this world, distinctions as regards contents as well as dimensions, of which we spoke in the first volume.[4]

What is polarity? To understand this law of polarity, the central importance of which for our whole understanding of reality has been clearly recognised by Schelling and Schleiermacher, we shall have to investigate a little further. What polarity is can be demonstrated most briefly, if we start from a

---

[3] Adolf Schlatter, *Das christliche Dogma*, Stuttgart 1911, p. 29f.
[4] *God Transcendent* (pp. 50-76).

distinction which we notice every moment, viz. the distinction
between rest and movement. Classical physics discovered the
law of the relativity of movement, as formulated by Leibnitz.
From a physical point of view rest and regular movement are
the same. A body is in movement only in relation to another
body that is at rest, or in relation to its own previous condition
of rest. Conversely a body is at rest only in relation to another
body that is in movement in relation to it, in other words which
alters its distance from it. Supposing all bodies in the universe
were to remain at the same distance from each other and
therefore not to alter their distance from each other, then one
could equally legitimately say "they are at rest", or "they are
in regular movement". Should one regard them as moving,
one could ascribe to them any speed one cared to choose, even
an infinite speed. The state in which the distances between all
the points remain unchanged we may call a state of indifference
between rest and movement, i.e. a state in which the contrast
between rest and movement is as yet non-existent. Rest and
movement balance each other. This balanced condition com-
prises both absolute rest and absolute movement. If we start
from this state of indifference, then the introduction of the contrast between rest and movement means a disturbance of the
original state of balance. The two, rest and movement, can
then be related only in a polar relation; consequently there is
movement only if there is also rest, and rest only if there is also
movement. They condition each other. The original state of
indifference ceases only when rest and movement, which in that
state were identical, fall apart as polar contrasts.

Polarity points back to the state of indifference in which the
contrast formed a unity. If we consider the change from the
state of indifference to the contrast, we see that two polar conditions come into being which are mutually related but which
must be distinguished clearly: (1) Rest and movement mutually
constitute each other, the state of rest existing only if the state
of movement exists and vice versa. (2) The entire relationship
between rest and movement can exist only because the original
state of indifference is in the background as its starting point.
This state of indifference need not be thought of as a state
which really did exist at some time. It is sufficient for it to be
conceivable. The contrast between rest and movement then

appears to be a cessation of this state of indifference. Therefore it is always conceivable that this contrast may return to the state of indifference. Consequently the distinction between rest and movement is a polar distinction because we can interpret it as starting from an *original* state of indifference and therefore as the breaking up or the differentiation of an *original* unity.

Polar relationship, which we have thus explained, therefore does not mean that the two given conditions which are related to one another in this way have any causal connexion, say e.g. by reciprocal action. Neither does it mean that they condition each other logically, like reason and consequences. Polarity is prior to all causal and logical relations. It is the *original* relationship in which all relations within the world more or less share. Therefore it cannot be deduced or explained from any of those particular relationships. It is *sui generis*.

As soon as by the elementary example of rest and movement we have made clear the principle of double polarity, we may gather that all distinctions within the world are conditioned by this contrast. All contrasts are merely variations on this theme, which we recognise everywhere once we have made ourselves acquainted with it. Every colour needs a contrasting colour before it becomes distinct as itself. But the spectrum of colours itself comes into being through friction of colourless light; all the colours of the rainbow are interdependent like points of a series. Again therefore we have the double polarity: (1) the contrast between two colours, the existence of each conditioning the other, and (2) the polar relationship between all colour contrasts and light, i.e. the state of indifference from which colour contrasts arise and to which they can return any minute. This state of indifference determines the existence of colour contrasts. The same applies to the light from which colours arise. This light is there only by contrast to darkness, i.e. against the background of a state of indifference in which the *original* light and the *original* night are identical. And the same also applies to sound. A tone is only there because of the tone interval, because of the existence of difference in volume and pitch. Behind all differences in sound there is an indifferent state of *original* sound which is at the same time the *original* silence – that which the Ancients called the harmony of the spheres.

All these distinctions, rest and movement, colour and contrasting colour, light and darkness, sound and silence, can,
according to modern science, be attributed to differences of
energy and ultimately to electrical processes. For not only light,
but also the matter of moving bodies, of material things,
previously regarded as at rest in themselves, have been reduced
to electrical charges which no longer have any bearer and the
restless movements of which constitute that which we perceive
as bodies. Contemporary atomic research has no unanimous
answer to the question, by what rules and in which courses
these fundamental components of the material world move.
But it is generally agreed that the chemical elements, i.e. the
component parts of the material world, are made up of electrical processes.

But then every energetic operation, and every electrical
charge only exists if there is a "tension of energy", in the words
of Sadi Carnot, i.e. an electrical charge which differs from the
"electric potential" of its surroundings. Only if there is a
tension between the thunder-cloud and the earth, i.e. if there
is a difference between their charges, do the surplus electrons
flash down to the earth to restore the balance, with the accom-
panying phenomena of light and sound.

Electric changes therefore happen only because of the existence of energetic differences which tend to level themselves out.
Then this causes new differences. We can see that if we throw
a brick into a pond. The rings of waves by which the movement
is forwarded are caused by the tendency to level up the contrast
which has disturbed the balance of the calm surface of the
water at the spot where the brick was dropped.

If therefore we regard the *original* process by which all bodies
of the empirical world are renewed from moment to moment
and new events arise in the world, then here too we are confronted with the same principle of polarity: (1) All operations
of power take place only if there is a contrast between two
energetic conditions. Power is available only as the overcoming
of resistance, as a contest with something else that is weaker
and by the overcoming of which power can be measured.
(2) The tension between two energetic conditions which alone
makes anything happen in the world is the elimination of the
balance of energy belonging to the *original* state.

It is usual to speak of the state of balance as a final state which everything endeavours to reach, in which the energetic changes that keep the world alive are increasingly levelled up and in which eventually even the contrast between heat and cold, into which at last all energetic distinctions will have turned, is levelled up by the dispersion of all available heat. This is the so-called "glacial death" of the world. We could just as well put this cessation of the world at the beginning and regard all bodies and all events in the world as a disturbance of this *original* state of balance. In this state of indifference infinite energy is the same as complete absence of energy, infinite heat the same as infinite cold, *original* light the same as *original* night, life the same as death. All energetic occurrences, all causes and effects through which events are carried forward, i.e. all causal connexions within the world, therefore exist only against the background of this state of indifference. We could conceive of them as having originated in an inexplicable interruption of this *original* state from which all that happens originates and to which it is to return as to its lost homeland.

The polar character of all distinctions within our empirical world, which we have made clear by these examples, becomes most clearly perceptible in practical life in the fact from which both Pascal and Schopenhauer started their pessimistic valuation of the human situation: any happiness that we can have in this world exists only by contrast to the suffering of the unsatisfied longing from which it promises to deliver us. Therefore pleasure lasts only as long as we feel the polar contrast with the suffering from which it has set us free. A drink refreshes us only as long as we still feel thirst. Rest is enjoyable only after strenuous labour. As soon as the desire is fulfilled, the aim is reached and we have forgotten the undesired condition, then satisfaction at once turns into boredom and weariness. Therefore a cause can make us enthusiastic only as long as it is still in conflict with undefeated enemies, as long therefore as we can feel the joy of victory again and again through the defeat of each enemy. But once the aim for which one has so enthusiastically fought has been reached, once all the enemies are prostrate and the longed-for state of undisturbed peace has come at last, then even the most glorious cause soon becomes tiresome. My volition and emotion therefore can be roused only by something that I do not yet have and that consequently as an attractive aim still lies before me, or by something that I have only just received and that consequently still has the attraction of a novelty. That which is no longer new does not hold me any longer. My desires are already looking further. We observe this in connexion with volition as well as with emotion.

Every aim which presents itself to my will, whether it is a large fortune or a house of my own, a safe position, world peace, or a class-free society, appears to me really worth aiming at only as long as it is still in the future which I can picture in glowing colours. But the aim is hardly reached before I begin to get weary of the cause. The will cannot find rest. That which has been reached merely serves as the starting point for a further aim which appears behind it. Admittedly the will does desire something in which it can find satisfaction and rest. But if it finds this, then, as Pascal observes, the abyss of inner emptiness and mortal boredom is again and again revealed therein. Repose becomes unbearable through the ennui which it begets, and the struggle, the chase, the game begins anew. This oscillation between rest and unrest is the fundamental constitution of our human life.[5] Every aim, as soon as it is reached, becomes the operational base for new and further aims. Our need of joy, our hunger for happiness keeps feeding only on coming joy, on the expectation of unheard-of happiness. If the expected pleasure really does come our way, then the short intoxication with delight soon gives way to disappointment. We are not satisfied. The same thing repeats itself: our thirst for pleasure passes what has been reached and hurries on to meet new pleasures which are still in the future. Therefore according to Schopenhauer our existence is an unceasing pendulum-movement between two conditions of feeling: pain and boredom. Pain as long as we do not have what we desire but only painfully long for it; boredom, loathing and weariness as soon as we have it and it has lost the charm of novelty.

Only now, after we have made clear the law of polarity by the contents of the material world, by movements of bodies,

[5] Cf. Blaise Pascal, *Pensées*, French edition with English translation by H. F. Stewart, London 1950, No. 116, pp. 56-65.

sounds, discharges of energy, and finally by the contrast of pleasure and pain, can we also discover it in the fundamental structures of our existence, viz. in the structure of time and of space, and in the dimensional relation between spaces, as discussed in the first volume. The extension of time, as demonstrated there, comes into being because there is the inexplicable contrast between the occurrence that is past and the occurrence that is present. Past and present are interdependent. There is a present only in relation to the past on which we look back from the present. The advantage which a current event has in being present is therefore possible only as the reverse of other events which are condemned no longer to be present but to be past. Conversely the same must be said about the past. There is only a past in relation to the present. For all that is past must have been present.

Because present and past mutually determine each other, a period of time, e.g. the hour of our life in which we are living just now, can only begin because the point at which it begins is at the same time also the end of a period of time which precedes it and which therefore is past in relation to it. A period of time therefore comes into being only because it is separated from another span of time. That is why an initial point of the entire course of time is simply inconceivable.

Causal connexion also shares in this polarity of time. If we trace an effect back to its cause, then we explain a present event by a past event. For the cause always precedes the effect. If therefore a starting point of time is inconceivable without its being the end of a preceding time, then it is also impossible for us to conceive of a cause which is not itself the effect of a preceding cause. We can also conceive this polar relation between that which is and that which was as the elimination of a state of balance in which the two poles were not yet separated.

That leads us to a thought which mystics have expressed continually: that there is an *original* condition in which no event has any precedence of time over another, a state of temporal indifference in which everything is present, *nunc aeternum*, and everything is past, in which in other words present and past are one in a higher unity.

The same holds good of space. A limited space, whether it

be an extent in space, like a railway track, or a piece of land, or a room, always comes into being because it is surrounded and bounded by another limited space. Every boundary upon earth where a new country begins is always a boundary where another country ceases. Every "here" is "here" only because there is a "there" with which it is in contrast. Space too with its contrast between different places can be regarded as the elimination of a state of indifference in which there is neither "here" nor "there", in which all places are united in one comprehensive omnipresent "here".

But what is true about time and space also holds good in respect of the final and most comprehensive fundamental forms of our existence, viz. the dimensional relation between spaces, using the word spaces in a general sense as defined in the first volume.[6] I am "I"[7] only in virtue of the objective space that confronts me and has to act as a foil for me before I can become conscious of being a knowing and willing "I". But the "it"-space too is objective space only as the object of a perceptive ego (*Ich*). This polar relationship of existing together and mutually determining each other of ego and object, as already shown in Vol. 1,[8] is not a causal relation. The "I" does not produce the world, nor does the world produce the ego. Neither is this a logical relation of reason and consequence. Subject and object rather confront each other in the *original* relation of polarity which is prior to any causal or logical relations and cannot be deduced from those particular relations. This polar relation exists not only between "I" and "it" but also between "I" and "thou". I am "I" only in relation to the "thou" that I meet. "I am only through thee."[9] My objective space exists only in contrast to your objective space.

In agreement with Indian mysticism we may regard those polar relations as the elimination of a state of indifference in which the distinction between "I" and "it", "I" and "thou" has been taken back in an ultimate *original* unity in which, according to Indian doctrine, the "three antitheses" of Knower,

---

[6] *God Transcendent* (pp. 60-1, 90).

[7] The reader should take special note of the subtle difference between the use of "I", "thou", "it" (*Ich, Du, Es*), in English as in German without declension, and I, thou, it (*ich, du, es*) etc. Tr.

[8] *God Transcendent* (pp. 103-52).   [9] *Op. cit.* (pp. 153ff).

Known and the act of Knowing have been annulled.[10]

It has been necessary to make such an extensive examination of the universal principle of polarity that gives to all relations in the world in which we are, to any distinctions which we make, however different they may be in other respects, their common character. Neither in reality nor in our mind is there anything that by itself would be what it is. All that we can perceive and imagine, in its existence as well as in its substance, in its quantitative as well as in its qualitative constitution, is qualified and determined by the existence of something else that confronts it as its opposite pole. We may, it is true, be able to pronounce and to write down the thesis: there is something that by itself is that which it is (*"id quod per se est id quod est"*,[11] *"id quod nulla alia re eget ad existendum"*[12]). But such words do not in fact convey anything. For with anything that we can imagine, whether it is a bodily thing or an event, a colour or a sound, a substance or a space, we always tacitly assume the environment from which it is distinguished, the correlate to which it corresponds and which determines its existence and substance (*Dasein und Sosein*). It is not possible to imagine a form which needs no other for its existence.

Fichte is therefore right when he declares: "The idea of creation cannot be conceived – at least not by anything which we can call thought! – nor has there ever been a man able to conceive it."[13] For we cannot imagine an initial link of the whole causal connexion, which exists by itself and produces all the other links. When we pronounce the word "Creator" we always visualise a human being who creates a form out of a given material, an artisan or a builder or an artist producing his work. The creative and formative activity of which a human subject is capable is always possible only because this subject with all his creative powers is the result of his ancestors, his nation, and the particular conditions of his life. Consequently it has been produced by a great number of prior causes. A man can be the starting point of a causal chain only because

---

[10] Rudolf Otto, *West-östliche Mystik*, Gotha 1926, p. 7; Engl. trans. *Mysticism East and West* by B. L. Bracey and R. C. Payne, New York 1932 (p. 3).

[11] Anselm, *Monologium*, 10, in Migne, *Patrologia Latina*, vol. CLVIII.

[12] Spinoza.

[13] *Glaube und Denken*, 3rd edn., p. 49 (41); Fichte, *Anweisung zum seligen Leben*, Berlin 1806, Engl. trans. *The Way to the blessed Life*, by F. Medicus, 1923, p. 89.

at the same time he is the end of a preceding causal connexion. A Creator in respect of whom this would not hold good is simply inconceivable to us.

The truth contained in the concept of creation, of which we shall speak later, is beyond all our human conceptions. It passes all understanding. This is caused by the polarity of all the distinctions which our mind makes. This polarity of all the decisions we make is the reason why all relations in which we stand are endless series in which we have to continue indefinitely one way or the other. This has nothing to do with a wild concept of infinity. We can still leave undecided the question whether the series in which we move are infinite. We only know that they are endless. We are unable at any point to wind up the extent of time or the series of causes and effects and to assume an initial or final point. For according to the law of polarity every initial point must be the final point of a preceding series and every final point must be the initial point of a new series.

CHAPTER 3

*The Reason Why it is Impossible for us to Lay Down
a Foundation of Life*

As we have now realised the structural law of our existence and of all our experience in its entire inescapability, it becomes clear that we meet with an insuperable barrier if we attempt to apprehend and to lay hold of God. For the moment we can see only that if God is, then this must find an expression in the incomprehensible halting of the unceasing movement with which we search for an ultimate cause of the world and an ultimate sanction of our actions, in our being confronted with a Power which silences the question, why it is there and whence it has the right to determine us. This halting of the question "why?", this wonderful silencing of the question "whence?" as regards the absolute obligation should not, however, be an act of force by which the question is crushed and gagged. It must not be a self-given order to stop short at this point or a mutual agreement not to ask or think any further beyond it. This would precisely not bring the question to a standstill. It would merely replace the question by a *sacrificium intellectus*. If the question regarding the cause of the world and the source of authority is really to be silenced, then this can happen only in one way: viz. by the removal of the reason for the unceasing movement, of that which keeps the questions "why?" and "whence?" in motion. This reason, as we saw, is the law of polarity to which everything within our empirical world is subject. Our question can therefore only come to a standstill in a condition which is no longer subject to the law of polarity, of which one can truly say that, as Anselm expresses it, nothing greater can be thought beyond it. But to our polar thinking this is a simply inconceivable thought. As soon as we attempt to imagine this condition, an image presents itself to our mind, not one beyond which we *cannot* think any further, but one beyond which we *will* not think any further. By our own effort or by mutual agreement we hold on to this image violently, though our mind aspires beyond it. What we gain in this way is in every case only that which Luther calls a self-created image (*figamentum*), a god "which they make and form for themselves (*deus, quem ipse sibi fingunt et formant*)", an "idol of their own heart (*idolum cordis sui*)". Luther calls this endeavour to create oneself a foundation of life by one's own effort *cognitio dei legalis*. This is the righteousness by works of the natural man which "makes bold to force our God down from heaven".[1]

This is not only the origin of the polytheistic ideas of God, of which Luther was primarily thinking. We should also understand this to include the Unmoved Mover of Aristotle and the ὀντῶς ὦν, the True Being, of Plato, and especially the philosophical idea of the Absolute in all its applications and variations, viz. the absolute ego, the absolute mind, the absolute spirit, the absolute reason. All these ideas are efforts of man to stop by a supposition of thought the restless movement and to escape from the relativism to which we are led by the polar character of all conditions which we can think. They are desperate exertions of our ego to jump over its own shadow and to pull itself out of the marsh by its own hair. Consequently in practical life these thought-images do not provide the slightest support. For if we want to hold on to them, we have to support them. In this way we do not get one step beyond the sphere of this world, even if we do speak of "the Word of God" or "the Absolute". Even if we do deify such an idea as our thought can assume and even if we are prepared to suffer and to die for it, it yet remains a purely this-worldly concern. It may perhaps not even contain the question concerning God. For as long as we try to make something do, that we can assume and create ourselves, we have avoided the difficult discussion of the question concerning God.

The religious confusion of ideas which at present has such devastating effects has come about through the very fact that the two things which the German Reformer has so clearly contrasted are continually being confused and being indicated by the same words. On the one hand the act of which we are all

---

[1] Vossberg, *Luther's Kritik aller Religion*, pp. 20ff; Luther, *Werke*, Erlangen edn., VOL. 13, p. 132.

capable, which indeed is a biological necessity to everyone of
us, the act in which we take a self-made starting-point of our
thought and action for absolute; and on the other hand the
act in which we have dispensed with all exertions and endeavours to provide ourselves with a foundation of life, and
through a purely passive act of receiving have found a ground
in which we can anchor our existence.

If we want to speak at all about this second possibility, which
is beyond our human reach, we can only declare that our
thought cannot arrive at this second possibility unless something
happens that puts our whole polar way of thinking out of
joint. For if there is an anchor-place for our existence which
we need not make and hold but which holds us, then this
means, describing it for the moment quite generally and ab-
stractly, that there is a Being which is not polar, which is
therefore not determined by anything else contrasting with it.
Only such a Being can put an end to the incessant movement
in which we are involved. If we say that God is the Being
that is beyond polarity, then we have as yet not made any
positive statement concerning Him and have not embarked on
any speculation concerning Him. We have merely denied, in
respect of God, what belongs to the character of all existence
accessible to us. We have therefore indicated the barrier
which separates all known reality from God. Indian wisdom
calls God "Him before whom words and thoughts return,
without finding". In the German language we indicate
this non-polar Reality by taking any word normally used for
a relation within this world and adding to it the undefinable
prefix "*Ur-*".[2] We speak of an *Ursein*, *original* being or existence; *Ursprung*, *origin*; *Uranfang*, *original* beginning; *Urwert*,
original value; *Urwillen*, *original* will; *Urkraft*, *original* power;
Ur-Du, *original* "thou". By this we mean a being that is the
origin of all that is and beyond which one cannot get any
further, as one can with the polar distinctions and conditions.
If there is an inconceivable and unthinkable *original* Being
that exists by Itself and is sufficient unto Itself, then there
follows an inevitable consequence which we shall have to draw

---

[2] There is no English equivalent for this prefix, but its meaning is clear in the
context. In the present book it is rendered *original* (in italics), except in such
expressions as *die Urgemeinde*, the early Church. Tr.

C

even if it does start from a thought which we cannot conceive.

Let us first try to draw the inevitable consequences without looking at the empirical world. This *original* Being that is by Itself cannot be beside or outside or opposite the world of which we are part. For otherwise there would again be a polar relation between It and the world. God would be the opposite pole to the world and His existence and substance would be determined by the world. If God is to be beyond all polarity then all that is must be in Him. The whole of reality must have its existence in Him. Wherever, in a way which we cannot comprehend, the genuine concept of God has appeared in history it has immediately been accompanied by that other thought: God bears all things within Himself. God is omnipresent in all things, in the smallest atom, at all places and at all times. All that happens is His work. God must be "everything to everyone" (1 Cor. xv.28).

All these statements are merely another way of saying that God is beyond all polarity. Only He who bears within Himself all that He is can be the ground in which our existence is anchored in every respect. For only He in whom all things are is the reality from which neither "I" nor "thou" nor anything at all can fall away. If anything at all existed which was not in God, then God would not be God but an object beside other objects, a power beside other powers, a space beside other spaces, something participating in that polar relation of tension which gives to all terrestrial reality its character. If anything at all existed that was beside or outside God, then the reality which surrounds us would consist of two parts: God and all the other things and beings which exist beside and outside God. Then I would not be in His presence and His sphere of power by the mere fact of my existence, then I could be outside Him and fall away from Him. Then I myself would have to do something and have to make an effort to remain in God. Then I would have to hold on to Him by my own strength.

Looking back, we have seen that only if there is a Reality which is not subject to the curse of polarity, only then does something exist in which our search for an ultimate sanction for our actions and an ultimate presupposition for our thought comes to a standstill. One more final consequence follows from this. If God is, then all that is, "I" and "thou" and all beings and all that exists around us, has a divine essence, a supra-polar *original* existence, inasmuch as it is in God, for God is the Being that is by itself, the comprehensive Being outside which nothing can be. All that is in God must participate in His essence. For if there were another non-divine being outside the divine Being, then this would be an opposite pole to the divine Being. That would make the divine Being itself polar. Then this would have a correlative by which its existence and substance would be partly determined. But that is contrary to the presuppositions from which we have drawn these conclusions.

Irrespective of our observation and of what we can imagine and think we have concluded all this from the statement – which we cannot think at all – that there is a Being that is not qualified and determined by something else outside It, as is the case with any objects we know. But if in view of this conclusion we reflect upon reality as it is given within us and around us we discover at once that it is in contrast to the statement we have just made. The reality of which we are part consists only of polar relations. The ultimate foundations and objects of trust which can be reached within it can be maintained only because in our own strength we make and suggest to others the decision that one must not go beyond them. So Alfred Rosenberg dictated at the time of Hitler: "the inner voice today demands that the myth of the blood . . . exclusively and without compromise must permeate, carry and determine our whole life"; "it tolerates no other supreme value beside itself."[3] Within the sphere of our world we can raise something to the level of a supreme value only in this tone of demand and intolerance. This corresponds with the polar character of our experience and of all our thinking, from which we cannot escape.

We are thus confronted with the insoluble contradiction between what has to be said about the *original* Being (*Ursein*), if we want to make any statement about it, and the fundamental structure of all reality within our reach. This contradiction cannot be expressed by finding the strongest contrasts which our language can express and then transposing these contrasts in the superlative and infinitely intensifying them and eventually in this utmost intensity applying them to the relation between God and the world, by saying e.g. "God reigns high

[3] Alfred Rosenberg, *Der Mythus des zwanzigsten Jahrhunderts*, Munich 1935, p. 83.

above our reach, He is above in Heaven and we are below on the earth", or "Between the Creator and the creature there is an infinite qualitative distinction." In this way the two manners of existence, the supra-polar divine *original* Being and the polar existence within our reach are admittedly contrary to each other but yet do not necessarily exclude one another. Even if they are infinitely removed from each other they can still exist together, in the same way as two stars 60,000,000 light-years apart can still exist within the same universe, or as two planes at right angles can yet exist within the same three-dimensional space. But this co-existence is the very thing that, according to what we have already said, is not possible for the divine and the earthly reality.

The contradiction to which we have been led seems to render the co-existence of the two impossible. In our reflexion we can express the relation which exists here only by an either-or. Either the world is "all in all" or God is "all in all". Either the world is all in all, i.e. there are only polar relations, and even that which people have always called "God" can be nothing other than an object amongst other objects, or a space amongst other spaces. Or God is all in all, and all that exists in the world is in God, all events in the world are God's work, the whole reality therefore in its real essence is *original* being and *original* event.

As we saw at the end of Vol. I this radical, insoluble and inexplicable either-or in which two mutually exclusive general statements concerning all that is confront one another is the third and final relation which, if God is, contains our existence. This third relation cannot be compared with the two relationships in which we stand within the world, i.e. with the qualitative and with the dimensional limit. Wherever genuine belief in God has existed – in such a way as we shall expound later – there people have at once experienced the insoluble either-or to which the concept of God leads. When men have been deeply affected by God they have known from the first moment that if God exists, then, with all our experience of the world and all our opinion of ourselves we are in conflict with Him. For if God is God then He must be all in all, everything to everyone. But the world consists merely of polar relationships of tension. Consequently God is not all in all.

It is impossible to bear with this contradiction in any way other than in the certitude that there will come a solution for which everything is heading and to which all believers look forward. "Eschatology", without which no genuine thought of God is possible, is the elementary expression of the fact that between God's existence and the existence of the world which we see around us there is an either-or that must be solved if we are not to perish by it. God must solve the polar existence of this world into His *original* existence, and then God will be all in all.

Without this burning expectation of the consummation genuine thought of God cannot live. The reality of a man's belief in God is shown exactly by the fact that he rejects every other solution of the contradiction as a false compromise. "May grace come and the world vanish" says the early Christian liturgy as described in the *Didache* (ch. x.6). Only when genuine belief in God relapses into rendering absolute what is relative, then the burning expectation of the future also vanishes and one begins again to make oneself at home in the world.

CHAPTER 4

The Non-recognisability of God

THE EITHER-OR between these two points of view is most clearly revealed when we ask the one question, in terms of which the impact of the "Christ message" becomes intelligible – namely the question how we can possibly have knowledge of God, seize Him, have contact with Him. If the world is all in all, if there are only relative truths, then that which we call God can also only be something relative that we have raised to the position of an ultimate value by our own decision and beside which we do not wish to tolerate anything else. This self-made object of trust is then naturally within reach of our knowledge, whether by a conclusion from this world to the "architect of the universe" or by a postulate from the action in which we are engaged to the ultimate meaning of this action. But if God is all in all, if there is therefore a comprehensive Being whom we have not raised to the position of a Supreme Value but who is by Himself the Value beyond which nothing greater can be conceived, then this Being is beyond the reach of our polar thought and knowledge. In other words we cannot see God. God's Essence is not merely hidden and invisible to our eyes in the sense in which the incandescent centre of our planet is hidden from our eyes, or the deepest spots of the Pacific, where no diver can reach the bottom of the sea, remain a hidden mystery. That would be only a relative concealment, and it would be conceivable that one day it might be surmounted by technical advances. But God is hidden and invisible to us absolutely.

All that we can perceive, conceive and think is therefore inside the endless series in which we are held as in an infinite prison. Consequently, if we look at the polar images which we can imagine we are looking in a direction opposite to God. For God is outside and beyond all polarities. We cannot make "any image or likeness" of Him. In other respects, it is true,

28

our reason, as Luther says, is "a great light" for which we can
never be sufficiently grateful. But it is blind when it is called
upon to recognise God's Being and consequently also our own
true essence and the real meaning of the world. "Reason may
raise and praise its light, and also be wise in worldly, temporal
things; but that certainly does not make it climb up into
Heaven, nor should one take its advice in things concerning
our salvation. For in this respect world and reason are blind
and will remain in the dark and not give any light for everlasting"; "therefore reason plays at blind man's buff with God,
and keeps doing the wrong thing and ever misses its aim, calling
'god' what is not God, and conversely not calling 'God' that
which is God, which it would not do if it did not know that
God is, or if it did know who and what God is. That is why it
comes to grief and gives the name and divine honour and calls
'god' whatever it thinks is God: but never meets with the true
God but every time with the devil or with their own conceit
which is governed by the devil."[1] Only afterwards, when
God's being has made itself known to us in a way which is
beyond our thinking, can we look back and recognise in our
benighted reason's mistaken ideas the mistakes of a mind which
is destined to communion with God. We then see that as long
as this mind has not found God, it must restlessly create, postulate and invent for itself an object of trust, and in so doing is
looking in the wrong direction. That is how it comes to the
deification of the creature.

Luther saw the inability of man to arrive at true knowledge
of God, even though in his day it was generally assumed that
the existence of God and His most important qualities were
accessible to reason through conclusions from nature, and even
though at times Luther himself reckoned with this possibility.
Now, in the era of secularism, the situation has become much
simpler and clearer. Wherever the spirit of modern natural
science and technology enters, it automatically drives out
the mythological images of gods and demons which made
natural occurrences appear to primitive man the work of gods
and invisible spirits. What is left are the visible and tangible
realities, the physical energies with which one can work

[1] Vossberg, *Luther's Kritik aller Religion*, pp. 31ff; Luther, *Werke*, Erlangen edn.,
VOL. 43, p. 353.

engines and can accomplish productive labour, and the
impulses and instincts by which the organic world lives. The
sense of realism of the present generation declines liturgical
celebrations and mythological imagery. One wants to see
actions and experience realities which have a practical and
tangible value.

To such an era there are only two possibilities left. The first
possibility is a conception of the world as depicted by Oswald
Spengler or Ernst Juenger. The whole of reality is a situation
of war, in which relative powers try each other's strength.
Spengler's realist-political picture of the situation of the world
in which he found himself, rests on the assumption that the
moving powers of the future are no different from those of the
past: the will of the stronger, healthy instincts, the race, the
will for possession and power; above this level dreams may
move to and fro without effect, dreams which will ever remain
dreams: righteousness, happiness, and peace.[2] To live therefore is to devote one's whole life to one of these fighting
powers, whether this be the Soviet system or a national movement or any other fighting power which demands our ultimate
devotion.

If one still has liturgical or mythical needs one can supply
this devotion, demanded by the inexorable course of events,
with a religious foundation or a theological support. One may,
for example, ascribe this pitiless struggle for existence, in which
everyone is left to his own resources, to a "creator" who from
the beginning has designed the world as an arena in which men
and nations in their struggle for power have to fight each other
with the sword. This religious and theological foundation may
still be a heart-felt need to the older generation and meet its
metaphysical inclinations, but it has no meaning for the man
who deals with realities, for the great politician or the economic
leader The division of powers on which he bases his calcula-
tions remains exactly the same whether we lay this religious
foundation or not. Consequently a realistic politician treats
the thoughts which people have about God as of no consequence. He leaves them alone as one leaves innocent things
alone as long as they do not interfere with the sphere of higher

---

[2] Oswald Spengler, *Der Untergang des Abendlandes*, Munich 1923; Engl. trans. *The Decline of the West* by C. F. Atkinson, London 1926.

politics. "Everyone shall be saved in his own way."[3] A politician bothers about religion only when it is necessary to curtail it, because some popular faith will not allow itself to be smoothly fitted into the struggle for power, as a fly-wheel is fitted into an engine to expedite its work. No, if faith in God has the courage to come forward out of its state of irrelevance and to interfere and disturb, then measures will have to be taken against it. But the way in which this is done shows that one does not take this faith seriously. One does not think it worth while going into the deeper causes that have led to the disturbance, but one treats it as a minor riot to which one sends out the police.

That is one possibility in the present situation. But there is another contrasting possibility. God ultimately is the sole Power to be reckoned with in all our human conduct, including all political acts and every economic enterprise. For if God is, then He is the One without whom nothing is that is. In every action He is not merely a power amongst other powers, a factor beside other factors which are in a polar relation to Him. No, but He is the Reality of all realities, the *original* Being, omnipresent in every atom as well as in every planetary movement, beyond all polar relations. Consequently God is involved in our struggle for power, as the One who works all in all, and on the other hand He is entirely beyond the struggle for power, as the *original* Power, by leaning on which at any point one can lift everything off its hinges.

For us as men acting responsibly in the present there are in every situation only two possibilities. Either God is against us; then we are godforsaken; in all that we undertake we then contradict our own true destination and all that we build we build on sand. When the rains come down and the winds blow and beat upon that house, it falls with a great crash (Mt. VII.27). Or God is with us. Then we stand on ground which has been laid without our effort. This foundation sustains us just the same when we are at the nadir of our existence as when we are being moved by a wave of enthusiasm and victory. If God is for us, then we have something that remains when our whole existence in this world of struggle for power is annihilated. Leaning on God we can resist all the world. He is the "Rock", the "sure Stronghold"[4] to which we can withdraw when every-

---

[3] Frederick the Great.   [4] Luther, Weimar edn., VOL. XXXV, pp. 455-7.

thing is against us and when everything that the world can give fails. When we die, at this lowest point of our life we do not fall into a blank but into God's arms. If in the world we become utterly poor we can be rich in God. If we are in a desperate situation, under the most terrible pressure, dishonoured and broken, with an excruciating death before us, like people condemned to lifelong forced labour in the Siberian "house of the dead", then we can still be happy in God in the midst of desperate suffering. If we are very weak, robbed of all bodily or physical strength, then God can be our strength. With God we can leap over a wall. "He who prays moves the arm that moves the universe."[5] According to the word of Jesus, he who has faith only as a mustard-seed, i.e. only a minimum of faith in God, can move mountains by virtue of that minimum of faith. Only if God is for us has our will an absolute binding, the power of which is absolutely superior to any influences within the world.

For we can never bind ourselves absolutely. Every obligation which we impose upon ourselves, every command which we give ourselves can fail at the critical moment when the sacrifice of our whole existence is demanded. For every command which we give ourselves we can also ourselves retract. Every obligation which we ourselves impose we ourselves can also abrogate. As soon as the self-chosen duty threatens to destroy us, it occurs to us to recall our decision. God alone can impose an obligation which we cannot cancel. For God is beyond the struggle which we fight for our existence. Nietzsche is right when he says: "Naïvety to think that any morality is left if there is no God to sanction it! The 'beyond' is absolutely necessary if a belief in morality is to be kept in being."

This is a word of great importance to every politician. Only God can make our will independent of any earthly wages and success and enable us, without any prospect of glory and recognition, as "unknown soldiers" gladly to give our lives for a cause which in this world is hopelessly lost. All this is possible only if God really is the *original* Being whom alone we have to take into account at every point of reality and who is yet beyond all the relations of tension which give their character to this world's struggles for power. It is only possible for God to catch

[5] Monod.

us up and bear us just when the situation is desperate and all our own energy is exhausted, if He is the *original* Power beyond all energetic tensions and struggles for power, superior in itself to any terrestrial power. If that is the case, then God is the power which must be taken into account as the decisive factor not only by the simple man of the people but also by the politician, the general and the industrial magnate in all his enterprises and measures. In spite of their mature political experience the late Roman Emperors made a serious miscalculation, when they thought they could by some violent measures quickly destroy the young movement of believers which arose from the lower classes of the population and disturbed their policy. They had not taken God into account for their policy and now they were amazed when they met with a Power which enabled weak maidens and children to face the lions fearlessly in the arena, a Power which proved stronger than all the measures which the Roman state commanded to suppress it.

With this we have shown the two points of view which are possible in the question about God and which now, in the era of secularism, are becoming more and more discernible: the one point of view according to which the ultimate meaning of our existence is merely the private and national struggle for power and for which therefore all religious ideologies have become irrelevant, and the other point of view according to which God is the *original* Power, whom alone we have eventually to take into account for every vital decision and leaning on whom alone we can fight with final devotion.

Only now, as we have contrasted these two possibilities, can we answer the question of God's recognisability in connexion with these two points of view. The answer follows from what has just been said. A god who is merely an expression for that on which we had already put our trust, is naturally within reach. We know what god is and what we have to do in his name, viz. precisely the same as we also do without him if we want to hold our own in the struggle in which we are engaged. This god does not disturb our sphere. He is never awkward to us because he simply confirms and emphasises what would be our main concern even if we did not have him. We are sure of this god and we never have that uncertain feeling that we should actually ask him first if he is agreeable to the use we make of him, and whether we have not maybe misunderstood him.

This secular idea of god has the great advantage that it is within easy reach and can easily be harmonised with what we would still deem the most important things in life if we did not have it. This advantage is, however, purchased by the disadvantage that a god whom we can so easily secure for ourselves has no meaning for our practical lives. He remains with us only so long as we are buoyed up on waves of enthusiasm and self-confidence. But he is not the rock on which we can stand firmly when all that is around us wavers and declines. Entirely different the God who is the Reality of realities, who is able to sustain us even at the lowest point of our existence. We can hold on to Him even if we have to despair of ourselves. But in order to find Him we have to bear the burden of a critical position in respect of God's recognisability which is so difficult that most people are not prepared to accept it unless they know that they must despair if they do not find God. For we are not able to see the God who is the anchor-ground of the soul and an everlasting binding of our will. All our perception, imagination and reflexion moves within polar relations. It has therefore no access to the *original* Being that sustains us. For That is beyond all polarity. What we can grasp by our cognition is always a dualism.

(1) We can stop the temporal and causal deduction from present to past, from an effect to its causes, from an action to its reason, and at this halting-place erect a product of the imagination, which we regard as the initial point in the series and raise to the position of an object of trust. In doing so we are seeking God. For we are seeking a place where the question "why?" and the question "whence our moral obligations?" come to a standstill. We do not find God in this way. According to Luther, in this way we do not reach God but an idol which we ourselves have to invent.

(2) But we can also do something else, which we are capable of doing by our own strength and which has in fact been done at all the culminating points of the history of religion. With our thinking and feeling we can return to the state of indifference to which all objects in the world, as we saw, have a polar relation. Man endeavours to find rest by submerging himself

in the state of balance which is the background of all those polar contrasts in which we find ourselves. Indian wisdom expresses this in the most elementary way when it says: God is *neti neti*, i.e. he is not that and not that, he is neither so nor so. He is the Being in which all the polar contrasts in the world are identical and annul one another.

Rudolf Otto in his book *West-östliche Mystik* has demonstrated that Sankara, Meister Eckhart and Fichte in wonderful agreement have often described this state of indifference by the same symbols, though they were quite independent of each other. Evidently a general human need has been active here, which is noticeable at all times and in all cultures but probably most strongly in the Aryan race. To describe the state which they have in view, they use again and again as a comparison the relation between the indifferent *original* light and colours. "Just as our physical eye is a prism, in which the ether, which is homogeneous, pure and colorless, breaks on the surfaces of things into manifold colors."[6] "This Being is simple, is like unto itself, unchangeable and unchanging; there is in it no becoming or ceasing to be, no change, or play of forms, but only the same quiet Being and Remaining."[7] But not only the inherent contrasts between colours and sounds but also the final dimensional relations between "I" and "it" are neutralised in God. The Eternal One is beyond the "three antitheses" of Knower, Known and the act of Knowing.[8] According to Yadjnavalkya one cannot say about God either that He exists or that He does not exist. And Eckhart says in exactly corresponding words: "If I say: God is a Being, this is not true: He is an exceeding Being and an *exceeding Nothingness*."[9]

Meditation, submersion in the state of indifference beyond any contrasts of content and dimension, has tremendous effects. This meditation is an old-established means of restoring the psychological balance in any situation. This is shown by the practice of Yoga, which has been used for thousands of years in Indian, Chinese and Japanese monasteries and has been increasingly perfected. From time immemorial people have

[6] R. Otto, *West-östliche Mystik*, p. 213 (225). Figures in brackets refer to the English edition.   [7] *Op. cit.*, p. 207 (220).   [8] *Op. cit.*, p. 7 (3).
[9] ed. F. Pfeiffer, *Deutsche Mystiker des vierzehnten Jahrhunderts*, Leipzig 1857, VOL. II, pp. 316-19.

believed that by a return to the state of indifference man manages to break the barrier of the plural world and to submerge himself in a sphere beyond all things.

But if what we said earlier about the state of balance is true, then this is precisely not the case. By such a return to the state of balance we have certainly left behind us the first polarity of relations of content and dimension. But this does not mean that we have left the polar world itself. We have merely retired from the first to the second polarity contained in this world, viz. the polar relation between every distinction within the empirical world and its dissolution in the point of indifference. Here too we are confronted with two elements which mutually determine each other, in other words which cannot exist by themselves. The state of balance is given only as the background and condition of the contrasts within the world; and the latter again presuppose the state of indifference at least as conceivable. The attempt of man to find rest in this state of balance therefore, just like the attempt to assume an initial link in a series of relations, is a violent exertion by which we try in vain, by our own effort, to liberate ourselves from the situation in which we are caught. By prolonged exertions and painful exercises one raises oneself, through an autosuggestion intensified to the utmost, to the thought that the state of indifference has actually been reached and that the restless process in which we have to move continually between unity and multiplicity has been brought to a standstill. But in fact the process is never brought to a standstill. As long as we live we are always forced to return from the state of balance to the contrasts of the world. What the mystic achieves is merely the ability to remain in the state of indifference longer than another man.

The efforts which man makes to conquer this final polarity too and to reach a conscious state of sleep in which the will to live ceases, deserve the highest admiration. It is the greatest chapter of the history of human religion. Nevertheless – from the point of view of Luther – exactly like the creation of an idol by violently arresting the process of relation, it is all man's own work, a cramped effort to jump across one's own shadow.

This exhausts the two possibilities open to us men, to find an answer to the question regarding God's essence. The whole history of extra-biblical religion is contained in those two possibilities. But the more seriously we walk those ways to the end, the more clearly we notice that we are facing an unsurmountable barrier. The *original* Being that we would fain grasp is not merely beyond all inherent and dimensional contrasts but – this knowledge is of fundamental importance – also beyond the second polarity between all contrasts in the world and the state of indifference in which the contrasts have been dissolved.

If we want to advance into the region which is not merely past the first but also beyond the second polarity, we are faced with the insoluble contradiction between two statements which are both necessary and yet mutually incompatible according to our polar cognitive faculty, to what Dostoevsky calls our "Euclidean intellect". (1) God is all in all, "from him and through him and to him are all things" (Rom. xi.36). (2) God is beyond all polar relationships, of which to our experience and our thought the whole world consists. We can therefore neither reach Him by means of causal deduction within the series of relations in the world, nor by returning from the contrasts of the world to their state of indifference.

If this incomprehensible God is the ultimate Reality, then all things and events, as Luther says, are God's "masks and disguises". If therefore we cannot comprehend God, then also access to the inner essence of the world and to the ultimate meaning of earthly events is closed to us. We can always only make the negative statement that the essence of things is something that does not have a polar character either in the first or in the second sense of the word. But the supra-polar mystery, which fills our own existence, the existence of other creatures and all nature, is beyond our capacity of comprehension. We have a presentiment of God in all things. We know that if God is, all events in the world are his work; but we cannot deduce its meaning from the polar superficial picture that we have of God's creation.

That is also why we cannot reach any certitude as to which way we should take, in which of the many directions of life we should walk if we want to live according to the ordinances of God's creation and fulfil our destiny. It is of course a small matter for us on our own responsibility to philosophise on the meaning of creation and from our superficial impression to come to ingenious and profound assumptions. But all these again break on reality. That is what happens, e.g. if we have seen the meaning of the created order in a lofty culture of humanity and now experience, without being able to discover any positive gain from such a work of destruction, a mass-catastrophe by which the incomprehensible Creator destroys again His own creation and takes away in the flash of a moment the most indispensable people He has brought into existence, or buries in one night under rubble and ash the most wonderful works of culture which He made men build in hundreds of years. It seems as if God forever defeats all our efforts to gather any meaning from His tremendous creating and destroying, like a teacher who destroys and rejects a concept which a pupil has put before him.

This knowledge about the insurmountable barriers which surround our thinking after all that has been said, the fact that we have been thrown out of the fancied security in which we made ourselves positive or negative ideas about the world, is the only condition that has to be fulfilled if we are to be in a position to listen to the message concerning Christ. We have not yet thereby become Christians, but our ear has been opened for the message. We are in the attitude which Jesus means when He says: "He that has ears to hear, let him hear!" As long as that negative condition has not been fulfilled, the message of the New Testament appears to us like the reply to a question which is no question at all, and therefore like "foolishness", like something not even worth while listening to.

This is merely a negative condition. But we cannot bring even that about by ourselves. We ourselves cannot leave the secular attitude in which we are imprisoned. If we are extricated from this position, then something has happened to us which, if we want to speak in a dogmatic way, we must already define as a revelation in the general sense of the word (*revelatio generalis*). This is our being made aware of the question to which we cannot ourselves find a reply, to which only God can give the answer, if there is any answer at all. When God has granted us an answer to this ultimate question of life, and when from there we look back on our lives so far, then it becomes clear to us that the awakening of the question to which we have now received an answer was already the work of the Spirit of God, even if the awakening of the question led at first to atheism because it destroyed all the images and thoughts of God which we had received from others or made ourselves.

This being thrown out of the security in which so far we have either denied God or too rashly asserted his existence can be put in motion by anything that happens in our life.

A man like Tolstoy, in the noontide of his life, at the height of glory and success, physically healthy and mentally fit, can be seized by the insoluble question: Why all these things – and what then? The question can also be aroused by a bewildering blow of fate which takes away everything that had given meaning to our life. The question of eternity can be set in motion by philosophical reflexion on the problem of infinity, as was the case with Pascal, or by the practical struggle for life on the battlefield of a World War. It can arise in the sphere of a highly developed religion like Islam or Buddhism, but it can also break out like a catastrophe in the midst of an atheist attitude. Whenever the great uncertainty strikes man, when the foundations upon which his life has so far been built start rocking, then he is able at least to listen for once to the message of Christ. For this message is addressed to men who know that in the ultimate question of life, in the quest for the Creator which gives our life its direction, we cannot guide ourselves.

PART TWO

THE SOVEREIGN AUTHORITY OF CHRIST

CHAPTER 5

Self-guidance or Guidance by Someone else

To UNDERSTAND the essence of Christianity we have to start from a fact that we have to acknowledge as historical even if we do not understand it or if we regard it as one of the most disastrous events in the history of Europe.

Christianity has come into being because a small but gradually growing group of people arrived at the certitude that there is a way in which we can be delivered of all vague notions of God and the burden of uncertainty as regards the mystery of the world. This way does not consist in trying to form a picture of God by deductions from nature and history, nor in sinking into the state of indifference in God by means of mystical contemplation. The way to certitude as regards God's essence and will consists in ceasing once and for all to guide[1] ourselves in this question and instead, with all our thoughts on the ultimate question of life and with all our decisions arising therefrom, resolutely submitting to the guidance of a Man whom God has destined to be the "Lord" of all of us who live after his appearance. This Man is Jesus of Nazareth.

If from our childhood we had not been accustomed to the language of the New Testament and its way of expressing itself, if instead we were to discover this book for the first time, then we would be struck more forcibly than we are now by the fact which in spite of all the differences as regards type of doctrine lends to the literature of the New Testament its common character, viz. the fact that we are here addressed by men who have resigned their claim to self-determination and have placed their lives in the hands of Someone else of whom even after His death they are convinced that He will be with them always even unto the end of the world. For the moment we can leave the question how the early Church arrived at the formula

---

[1] "Guide" and "lead" are used (almost, though not entirely indiscriminately) to render the same German word, *führen*, which means both. Tr.

"Jesus is Lord" (κύριος Ἰησοῦς, 1 Cor. xii.3), by which, under the influence of its surroundings and of the Septuagint, it expressed from an early age the relation in which it stood to its Master.

For the moment the important thing for us is to consider the inner attitude that led to this confession. The men who speak to us in the New Testament know that from a certain day in their lives onward they have been called by that other One. He has invited them to walk behind Him during the whole of their lives and to follow in His footsteps. If they are persecuted on account of that they do not die on their own responsibility; they carry their cross behind Him. They are the people "who follow the Lamb wherever he goes" (Rev. xiv.4: οὗτοι οἱ ἀκολουθοῦντες τῷ ἀρνίῳ ὅπου ἂν ὑπάγῃ). When they greet each other or when they rejoice, they do this "in Him". When they have hurt each other and make peace, then they forgive each other "in the presence of Christ" (ii Cor. ii.10). They know that they are members of His body. Their movements therefore are guided by Him, as the movements of a man's hand, or the steps which he takes are guided by his will. They die "with Him" and are brought to life again "with Him", thereafter to be "with Him" forever.

If this being guided by someone else, of which the first Christians speak, really extends to the whole of human life, then it cannot be limited to volition and action. It must also include the other side of human existence: cognition. Therefore the men who speak to us in the New Testament have manifestly also placed their whole thought-life in the hand of this other One. The questions as regards the meaning of creation and the *original* ground and ultimate end of events in the world cannot be solved by speculating and having one's own ideas on these things. As far as these ultimate questions of our knowledge can be answered at all, they receive their answer by the fact that within the "body of Christ", guided by the Spirit of Christ, which is the Church, there is according to i Cor. xii.8 also a "Word of wisdom" (λόγος τῆς σοφίας) and a "Word of knowledge" (λόγος τῆς γνώσεως), as a gift of the Spirit which no one can obtain for himself. When Paul, in the Epistle to the Romans, chapter xi, looks into the design of the history of the nations, he communicates what he has seen to the Church as a mystery (μυστήριον v. 25) that has been revealed to him. The prologue to the Gospel according to John and the first chapters of the Epistles to the Ephesians and the Colossians are examples of philosophical thought under the influence of enlightenment by Christ. What they have grasped of the ultimate meaning of nature and history has been revealed to them by Christ, and they do not desire to probe into that which He has still concealed from them because they "cannot yet bear" it.

Before we discuss what the other One, in whose hand those people have placed their thinking and their willing, has to tell us, and what is the effect of His guidance on all aspects of life, what it means to our theological knowledge and how from there questions as to the meaning, the guilt, and the future of the world are solved, we must first consider the fundamental attitude which has now been characterised as the key to the solution of all our problems and which consists in this: that we have given the guidance of every aspect of our life into the hand of someone else.

In his Shorter Catechism, in the explanation of the second article of faith, in the tremendous thesis which has been called the most beautiful phrase in the German language, Luther has made all that he said about the salvation and the consummation of the world by Jesus Christ dependent, in one prolonged relative clause, on the one statement from which it naturally unfolds: "That Jesus Christ . . . is my Lord." What Luther means by that is made clear by a statement in another context: "Christ is my immediate bishop, abbot, prior, Lord, Father and Master; I know no other."

The attitude meant by this, being under the guidance of someone else, is manifestly contrary to the other fundamental attitude which we all adopt by nature and which is common to nearly all non-Christian systems of life: the attitude in which we guide ourselves. If I guide myself, this does not mean that I have produced the end which determines my will. It is quite possible that the purpose of my life, e.g. the national community to which I devote myself, or the progress of civilisation to which I contribute, or whatever else it may be, is something that I have not myself created. I may have received it as a gift in the cradle when I was born.

But the important thing for the guidance of my life is not the origin of the purpose whic   determines my will, whether I have designed it and thought it out myself or whether I have received it from elsewhere. The only question is: whence does it receive its validity? For even if I have inherited it from my fathers or have received it as an aspect of my character it does not necessarily follow that it must be the foundation of all my decisions. I might also have the heavy task of renouncing all that I have, wrenching myself with a thousand pains from the native soil from which I have grown and in which I am rooted with every fibre, allowing myself to be transplanted into another world. If I do not find this necessary but on the contrary plant my roots as deeply as possible into my native soil so as to get strength from it, is not this position indicated to me simply because I have already found myself in possession of those values? For only now does the question arise: should I renounce those values – like Paul "count them for loss and refuse" – or should they remain in force forever?

The position (*Stelle*) from which this question is decided is the authority (*Stelle*) by which I am guided and to which I look up when I am faced with values which want to determine my life. There are only two possibilities. Either I lead myself, I think on my own responsibility and I myself choose the values which are to regulate my future. Or I am led by someone else.

First of all let us consider the first, most obvious possibility. As long as I guide myself, the values applied therein can be of various kinds. In itself anything can become the foundation which I arrange for my own life, whether I have made it myself, or whether I have received it from elsewhere. Only one thing is excluded. That is the other "I" to which I can enter into a relationship of "thou". For a "thou" is the only reality which I can never possess. I can take possession of a thought expressed by someone else, of an order which he has given, of a programme which he has drawn up, and make it applicable to myself. But I can never take possession of him. I have access to him only in so far as he discloses himself to me. As long as I guide myself I can make anything the foundation of my life, except another ego. That by which I live must therefore remain outside the "I-thou" relationship.

Within this limit there is however a great number of possibilities. I mention only the most important ones. The foundation on which my life rests can be the entire objective reality. I plunge into the ordinances of life and the laws of development by which the whole course of the world so far has been governed. I trust myself to the powerful stream of reality and let myself be carried by it. I make no attempt to go against the stream. The Stoics called that *secundam naturam vivere* (living according to nature). They were thinking of the never-changing laws of nature. In the nineteenth century the foundation of life to many people was not so much the immutable order of nature but the agitated reality in its development. Men wanted to collaborate in the rise of the world and the cultural progress of mankind. The objective reality to which they trusted themselves seemed no longer to be a mechanism moving according to immutable laws, but a growing organism, laden with unlimited possibilities.

It does not matter whether I surrender to an immutable or to a changing reality; as long as I base myself upon reality, without ever asking what justifies my confidence in it, I am guiding myself. For this surrender to the fundamental ordinances of the course of the world is not the only possibility open to me, I could also rebel against those ordinances. If I do not do this, I am not forced by circumstances but it is I myself who have made and make repeatedly the act of faithful surrender to reality. Either by a conscious decision or by an unconscious strong impulse I myself must have repeatedly decided to affirm reality in its present form.

A second form of self-guidance consists in having a rule of conduct, e.g. an extensive written law, a monastic rule or a code which orders and encompasses the whole of our life. In most cases such a law will consist of maxims which we have not made ourselves but are commanded by another. Even so we do not come under another man's guidance. For the command can be abstracted from the "thou"-relationship to the lawgiver. I can live according to his law without even knowing who he is. It has been abstracted from the lawgiver and has become an independent, self-sufficient entity which I can possess without being dependent on anyone.

Another form of self-guidance consists in having a programme for the future to collaborate in, an idea to guide me, or an ideal in view, an abstract value or scale of values by which I find my bearings. Ideas and programmes of world reform have always been originated, expounded and embodied by some individual, but their validity is independent of these men, just as euclidean geometry is independent of the first man to discover it. I can live by these thoughts without entering into a "thou"-relationship, just as I can walk across a bridge without knowing who built it.

In all these forms of self-guidance a great historical personality can play an important part. He may be the prophet who first sees the programme for the future. He may be Copernicus or Euclid, to whom we owe a truth. He may have exercised Socratic midwifery and brought the sleeping memory to the daylight of consciousness. Nevertheless the value which I owe to such a discoverer or prophet is not like a planet which every moment receives its light anew from the sun, which would immediately lose its light if the sun were not there or had lost its power. This value is more like a fixed star which shines by its own power. It needs no "thou" from which to derive its illumination.

In contrast to all these forms of self-guidance, however rich and manifold, is the attitude which, according to the witness of the New Testament, can alone save us from the nihilism which is the inevitable outcome of all efforts which we men make to guide ourselves. If I no longer guide myself, if my fate is in the hand of Someone else who is my Lord, decisions can be made which indeed to a very great extent, seen from without, seem very much the same as those made in the contrasting attitude of self-guidance. The same commandments and values can come into force, values like the order of nature or the nation or the brotherhood of man. But the authority which establishes them is different. It is no longer within my jurisdiction, whether these values are repeatedly put into force or not. I live in the presence of Someone else. Before Him all values are every moment weighed in the balance. From moment to moment He decides how much weight they should have for me. If He so desires He can at any time sovereignly dispose of such an undisputed and acknowledged foundation of our existence as the relationship of the family, and say: "If any one comes to me and does not hate his own father and mother and wife and children and brothers and sisters, yes, and even his own life, he cannot be my disciple" (Lk. xiv.26). He can forbid the man who wants to follow Him, to bury his father.

Paul pithily expresses this new foundation for our lives, when we give up the effort to guide ourselves and come under the sway of someone else, when he says he has become ἔννομος Χριστοῦ, "under the law of Christ" (1 Cor. ix.21). The Jewish *Thorah*, his rule of conduct so far, has been replaced by a living norm, Christ.

This dependence on a living ego instead of a rule of conduct at our disposal is expressed in the Gospel according to John, when among many "I"-words Christ pronounces the thesis, which the first hearers found so particularly difficult to understand: "I am the way." The place, occupied for the ordinary man by the way of life, the prescribed direction, summed up in some rules, aims and ideas, is now taken by something quite different, viz. an ego that demands that we shall follow it wherever it goes. Christ does not merely want to be the one who makes the street and builds the bridge: He himself is the street and the bridge. He is the way.

Whenever the New Testament witnesses speak of the Kingdom, the Lordship of Christ, which they experience as something new and unheard-of, the contrast becomes manifest between this being guided personally and any other kind of guidance to which they had been accustomed. This being guided excludes all other forms of shaping our lives. Here no "as well as" is possible, but only an "either-or". When Paul describes the great change which he has experienced under the influence of Jesus, he expresses in the strongest terms which he knew how to use, how valueless all that so far was gain to him has become since "being in Christ" presented itself to him as the new great possibility for us men. Circumcision, racial purity, the heritage of his tribe, pharisaism, blameless fulfilment of the law, these he says, I counted as loss for the sake of Christ. "Indeed I count everything as loss because of the surpassing worth of knowing Christ Jesus my Lord. For his sake I have suffered the loss of all things, and count them as refuse, in order that I may gain Christ and be found in him" (Phil. iii.7-9).

This exclusive contrast between guidance by Christ and other values and norms does not depend on inherent differences between the actions performed in either case. Jesus can order something that is pure fulfilment of Old Testament requirements. He can refer back to an ordinance of creation as in the case of the question of divorce. Nevertheless the action has an entirely different content when it is done for His sake, as compared to when we obey a commandment or an order for its own sake.

That guidance by Christ is incompatible with any other guidance is not because self-guidance is liberty and responsibility while guidance by Christ is slavish dependence, the obedience of a dead body, penal servitude and renunciation of one's own personality. Paul, it is true, calls himself again and again a slave ("servant", R.S.V.) of Christ in order to express in terms of the ancient order of society the dependence in which he stands before Christ. But just as frequently the service of Christ – as contrasted with the slavery of the law, of sin and of one's ego – is to him the great liberation of man from all coercive relations, salvation to a life of inner spontaneity. "Where the Spirit of the Lord is, there is freedom" (II Cor. III.17). In His service we are granted a look into "the perfect law, the law of liberty" (Jas. 1.25). For – we shall have to speak about this more explicitly later on – in Christ the hidden meaning of creation is revealed to us. His commandments therefore are no acts of oppression, imposed on us from without. When Christ comes to us, He comes "unto his own" (Jn. 1.11 R.V.). When He speaks, then our hidden nature, concealed even from ourselves, is disclosed to us.

CHAPTER 6

The early Christian Confession "Jesus is Lord"

THAT THE SERVICE of Christ excludes every other guidance of life is caused neither by the different content of His instructions as compared to all other programmes of conduct, nor by the distinction between freedom and coercion. It simply follows from the character of guidance. For whatever historical religious roots the New Testament idea of leadership or "Lordship" may have, at all events it belongs to the essence of Lordship or authority, that guidance can always come from only *one* authority and never from two or more at the same time. This has been unmistakably made clear by Jesus' word about the impossibility of double service: "No one can serve two masters; for either he will hate the one and love the other, or he will be devoted to the one and despise the other" (Mt. VI.24).

The king of a constitutional monarchy or of a country with parliamentary government, who needs the counter-signature of a ministry or the approval of parliament to give out an edict, is therefore no "Lord" in the full ancient sense of the word, which Jesus here presupposes. For in these modern forms of constitution leadership does not come from one authority but from more than one at the same time.

If Jesus is for us Lord in the unequivocal sense in which He himself uses the word in the Sermon on the Mount, then His ruling authority cannot be used as a court of appeal to reinforce the independent judgments of a lower court. For then guidance would not come from one authority but from two added together. Therefore if Jesus is the Lord then He must first validate every norm and every value that applies without Him. We cannot, for instance, start from an ordinance of nature which would be valid for us independently of Him, and then allow Jesus' instruction to be added afterwards as completion and confirmation of something which we already know. We should thus be trying to serve two masters and have ceased to acknowledge Jesus as the Lord. For if He is the Lord, it is for Him alone to decide which natural laws really are "ordinances of creation".

Nor can we interpret Jesus' instructions in the light of a picture of our human existence drawn independently of Him. For if He is the Lord, then only He can disclose to us our real essence. Neither can we begin by acknowledging the history of the world before Jesus, or a part of it – e.g. the history of Israel as recorded in the Old Testament – as God's revelation and then come to Christ and regard Him as the One who concludes and intensifies the history of revelation. We may then be believers in a revelation but we have not acknowledged Jesus as the Lord; we have made the impossible effort to serve two Lords. For if Jesus is the Lord then a part of history before Him or a record existing prior to His appearance cannot contain any revealing value independently of Him. To us who belong to Christ it can only be put in force by Him. For guidance can always only come from one authority, not from two at once.

A second, equally self-evident, characteristic of leadership, is connected with this. I can only be guided by someone who is contemporary with me. Only a contemporary can command me. From someone of the past I can receive commandments, rules of conduct, programmes, values, aims, make them my own and put them in force for myself. If I do that, however, I am not guided by him but guide myself. For all that I receive from a personality of the past, whether it is an old property or a principle or a programme of conduct, is an "it" which I "experience and use", which in other words I have in my power. As long as I am dealing only in an "I-it" relationship with objects, I am still ruling myself. I have not yet put my life in the hand of someone else who disposes of me.

This is possible only in an "I-thou" relationship, which presupposes contemporaneity. If this is true, then the confession "Jesus is Lord" cannot possibly be asserted as a supra-temporal generality, but can only be made by men living at a particular time who are convinced that Jesus lives at the same time and speaks to them as a contemporary. That is why the Epistle to the Hebrews makes a clear distinction between the present time in which God speaks to us who live now through Christ as the

Lord authorised by Him, and the past in which God had spoken to previous generations through men who lived then. "In many and various ways God spoke of old to our fathers by the prophets; but in these last days he has spoken to us by a Son" (Heb. 1.1).

If therefore we acknowledge Jesus to be our Lord, it is still possible for people to have lived, before His appearance, under other leaders who were their contemporaries as Jesus is ours. But what was possible before the appearance of Christ is no longer possible to us who live in the era of Christ. God speaks to us "by a Son". The words which the prophets spoke to the "fathers" are made valid to us only because the present Christ "opens to us the Scriptures" (Lk. xxiv.32). For there is leadership only if the Leader and those who are being led meet one another on the level of the present, in other words if they are contemporary.

We have seen that there are two essential characteristics of leadership, which follow from the simple meaning of the word "Lord": (1) Leadership can come only from one authority, never from two authorities at once. (2) The Leader must be a present "Thou" contemporary with those who are being led. This result is confirmed by the inquiries which have lately been made into the origin of the early Christian confession "Jesus is Lord".

Since the publication of Bousset's work *Kyrios Christos* the meaning of the confession "Jesus is Lord" has been the object of lively discussion in which Deiszmann, Kattenbusch, Boehlig, Althaus and Werner Fœrster have taken part.[1] With some reservations we are now in a position to say that although in Mark's Gospel Jesus is called the Lord only once, and that by the Syro-Phoenician woman, yet it is impossible to agree with Bousset's thesis that this expression arose in the Hellenistic church at Antioch and that it could only apply to a divine being which had become the centre of a religious society and around which a cult-legend had developed. The Aramaic expression *Maranatha*, which is used by Paul (1 Cor. xvi.22)

---

[1] The latter in his exhaustive study "Herr ist Jesus" in *Neutestamentliche For- schungen*, ed. Otto Schmitz, VOL. II, No. 1. Cf. also Werner Fœrster's article κύριος in *Theologisches Wörterbuch zum neuen Testament*, ed. Gerhard Kittel, Stuttgart 1932-, VOL. IV, pp. 1038ff.

and which also occurs in Greek ἔρχου κύριε (Come, Lord!) in Rev. XXII.20, and the expression "brother of the Lord" clearly point beyond the church of Antioch to Jerusalem. The title certainly does occur in the Mystery religions, e.g. in the cults of Mithras, Serapis and Isis, but by no means so often and so exclusively as one might expect. Where it occurs it seems to mean simply that the divine being calls the myste to its service and the latter has to obey it in all things, as is shown by the vivid picture by Apuleius in the *Metamorphoses* BK. XI, where we hear again and again of *imperia, nutus, monitum, iussus, obsequium, servitium, iugum*: commands, orders, exhortation, bidding, submission, service and yoke. The myste has taken on himself a heavy service, which mainly consists in the avoidance of certain foods and other abstemiousness, and in obedience to the command of the goddess who makes herself known through dreams and through the mouth of the priest.

The nearest parallel to the application of the word "Lord" to Jesus seems to be the cult of the Roman Emperor, because here an actual man is called the lord, rather than a deity in the sense of the mystery religions. But it is highly disputed whether the word *kyrios* or *dominus* when applied to the Roman Emperor is intended to characterise him as a divine being. Suetonius informs us that Augustus expressly declined the title *kyrios* because he did not want to describe his subjects as slaves. To call the Emperor *dominus* seemed to the free Roman citizen base flattery, unworthy of a Roman. The official cult of the Emperor was not directed to the *kyrios* but to the *sebastos*, the object of reverence. When Christians were executed because they rejected the cult of the Emperor, it was not because they had denied him the title of "lord". When Nero's cupbearer Patroclus was converted to Jesus, and the Emperor asked him: "Patroclus, do you now fight for that King?", he answered: "Aye, my lord Caesar (ναὶ κύριε καῖσαρ)." Thus it was not the title of lord that was objectionable to the Christians – they could use it without prejudice in a purely profane sense – but only the sacrifice demanded of them.

The fact that, according to Suetonius, Augustus declined the title of "lord" as unworthy of a free Roman shows clearly that at that time the word primarily indicated a master's ownership of a slave. The profane use of the word in those days therefore points in the same direction as the use of the word in the Gospel parables. *Kyrios* in both cases indicates the unimpeded possession of things, animals and slaves. It means in the first place the master of a house with domestic servants. It is the same when Jesus says: "Why do you call me *Kyrios* and not do what I tell you?" (Lk. VI.46). Disobedience therefore is contrary to the idea of the "lord" whose property the slave is and to whom he owes unconditional obedience.

In Eph. VI.5-9 it is said that slaves are to obey their lords, and then that lords also have a Lord to whom they owe the same obedience which they expect from their slaves. Consequently Paul especially prefers the expression *Kyrios* when he refers to commandments issued by the Lord, e.g. in I Cor. VII.10, 12, 23 in connexion with marriage, and I Cor. IX.14 in connexion with the question whether the witnesses of the Gospel ought to earn their own subsistence.

It points in the same direction that according to Acts XVII.7 the message of the Apostles concerning the "Lordship" of Christ could be misunderstood to the effect that they wanted to say that someone other than the Roman Emperor, namely Jesus, was the King whom all the world should obey.

It is in this light that one should understand the connexion with the Old Testament name of Jahveh, to which Bornhäuser attributes decisive importance when he says: "The way in which, as a matter of course, without any preceding explanation, Old Testament texts which refer to Yahveh, are applied to Jesus, proves that this is the meaning of Ἰησοῦς κύριος."[2] If by the word *Kyrios* an authority is attributed to Jesus which belonged to Yahveh in the Old Testament, then after all that has been said this can only mean that God has conferred on Jesus the ruling authority which is proper to Himself, so that all men owe Him absolute obedience. This is expressly stated in I Cor. XV.25ff. It is said there: "God has put all things in subjection under his feet." It was not like that from the beginning and it will not always remain so. But for a certain time God has conferred on Him the highest authority. In this time the aim appointed for this present age will be reached: that before Him every knee shall bend and every tongue confess

---

[2] K. Bornhäuser, *Zum Petrusbekenntnis und zur Hohenpriesterfrage*, Gütersloh 1921, p. 80.

E

that He is the Lord. At the end of this time He will return the dominion to God.

Therefore, whether we explain the worship of the *Kyrios* by the mystery religions, or quote as a parallel the cult of the Roman Emperor, or go back to the language of the Septuagint, which translates the name of Yahveh by κύριος, all these explanations consistently point in one direction: the *Kyrios* is the owner and master who has an unqualified authority over those in his service. Only one can exercise this "Lordship", never two at once, because it includes a total claim; and this one must be a contemporary, because service implies an "I-thou" relationship.

Because of the experience of the demonic distortion of leadership which we have had in the national and political field we are better prepared than previous generations to understand what the Early Church meant by the dominion of Jesus. What we experienced in Germany and of which we still retain the terrible memory, did not claim to be a leadership embracing our entire existence, in the full sense of the New Testament word "*Kyrios*". Nevertheless our generation is readier for an understanding of the fundamental attitude of early Christianity, than the era of Rationalism and the time of German Idealism, because in a field that seemed to give thousands of people a new fulness of life, it has received a negative demonstration, in the form of a sinister misleader, of the nature of leadership and the fact that we need leadership because we are not able to lead ourselves. Here was made clear, though by a terrible caricature, the exclusive contradiction between a position under guidance and every other form of life in which we direct ourselves to impersonal values. For the unheard-of suggestiveness of this personal leadership was closely connected with the fact that by the end of the first World War we had landed in a crisis of all impersonal values, ideas and philosophies unprecedented in the history of the human mind. The more catastrophic the devaluation of all those values, the stronger became the need of the genuine leader, the more the mind could be prepared for the particular character of this new immediate obligation, as compared to which, according to Paul (Phil. III.8), all values in life which had shone for him, disappear in the shade.

It is staggering to read how Edwin Erich Dwinger depicts,

in his war-book *Zwischen Weiss und Rot*, the internal catastrophe which overtook previously accepted ideas in the fateful period after the first World War, and the resulting vacuum. Some German prisoners of war are travelling home hopelessly across the Asiatic steppes. The Berlin artist approaches the ensign: "Tell me, *Fähnrich*," he says, "do you remember what Bockhorn, our good doctor, said to us at Kotzkoye on Christmas Eve? He made a little speech, but I can only remember that it was fine, and if you . . .?" – "Yes, Hatschek, I can! He said: a man who is not able to sacrifice himself for an idea, no matter what, is not yet a man in the full sense of the word, has never yet got beyond the animal stage. Here we are doing the one thing that makes a man – suffering for an idea. . . ." – "Yes", Hatschek then said, "he was right, our doctor Bockhorn! At the time I did not yet understand, it was, so to speak, too high for me. . . . Words, I thought, fine words – a new shirt would be more useful! But now I understand, you know . . . yes, it was so easy then, because we had what he said – an idea or something. . . . It is much more difficult now, because we have nothing left . . . nothing to hold on to! And so I would like to ask you: can't you give us something of the kind, that Bockhorn said? An idea or suchlike, you know, which would make things easier for us, for which we could bear all this better . . .?" He then goes on to say that this is the most terrible thing that can happen to a man: to suffer without any meaning. If we have no idea left for which to suffer, then our pains become ten times as bad. The ensign, thinking what he can say to make the situation somewhat easier for his companion, eventually hits on the idea: "We are suffering here so that other people in later times need not again suffer so terribly." But he feels that this thought is not strong enough to support his companions' heavy burden. He experiences the vacuum that is left by the fading of the last ideas by which one had lived at the time of the first World War.

The emptiness left after the end of the first World War by the disappearance of the whole world of ideas belonging to Rationalism, the French Revolution and German Idealism, was filled by a new conception which was to take the place of all ideas and programmes as an invisible factor of power: the experience of leadership. Since then great movements have no

longer been impelled by ideas, they crystallised round a man
with qualities for leadership like Lenin, Gandhi or Mussolini.
What made the leader a leader was no longer his blue blood,
his royal descent, his glittering court. Neither was it a title, a
rank or an office. Nor was it achieved by money or by connexions with the *haute finance*. What set millions in motion so
that they crowded together, as soon as the leader spoke, what
called thousands up, so that they put themselves unconditionally at his disposal was not something that could be abstracted
from his person. It was only himself, *"il duce"*, *"der Führer"*.
What made him the leader was not the programme that he
promised to carry out, nor the philosophy or the moral system
which he represented. For that might be abstracted from himself. True leadership depends only on the person of the leader.
Where there is real leadership the led attach themselves to the
leader unconditionally. They have infinite confidence in him.
They do not ask him to bind himself to a programme for the
future. They need his command for the present. They do not
need to know what is to happen tomorrow. They have once
and for all "jumped into the fiery circle of his leadership",
have bound themselves to him for life and death and are at his
disposal. He has their fate in his hands.

The only question is, was this experience of leadership,
which gave the whole period after the first World War its character and before which all the old ideas and norms seemed to
disappear in the shade, truth or mass-suggestion? In the mean-
time – as we have already said – we have experienced a misleader of extraordinary stature, in whom millions of people
believed they had found the fulfilment of their longing for
genuine leadership. Now we Christians at any rate know that
the whole thing was a satanic temptation on the largest scale.
We know now that in the political field no man has the authority
to gather into his own hands the total guidance of an entire
nation or the whole human race itself. Every effort towards
this end must rob the people who submit to it of their independence and so of their human dignity. In the long run this does
not only lead to a political catastrophe, but also paves the
way for antichristianity. The fact that we have experienced
this in our own lives makes us perhaps more prepared than
previous generations for what the Early Church meant by the

Lordship of Christ. From the negative distorted image of a satanic leadership we are in a better position than previous generations to recognise the essence of genuine leadership as we meet it in the New Testament, in Paul's statements concerning the κύριος and the κύριοι. This religious-political leader-worship of recent times has the same relation to the dominion of Christ as the pagan *kyrios*-worship which at the time of the ancient Christian world-mission was spreading round the Mediterranean in many forms; in the worship of healing deities like Aesculapius or Serapis, or in the apotheosis of men, expressed in the paean with which Demetrius Polyorketes was welcomed in Athens: "Thou art the *kyrios*!" Paul is deliberately using this worship of lords as a means to make the dominion of Christ understood, when he says: "For although there may be so-called gods in heaven or on earth – as indeed there are many 'gods' and many 'lords' (*kyrioi*), yet for us there is one God, the Father . . . and one Lord (*Kyrios*), Jesus Christ . . ." (i Cor. viii.5-6).

The worship of lords therefore had created a category of its own, the category of the *kyrios*. And this category finds its fulfilment in Christ.

There can be only one true Leader. The secret of his leadership can be experienced in its depth only by surrender to Him. Nevertheless our negative experience of false leaders can suggest to us an understanding of what the New Testament attests as regards the Leader's authority of Jesus. We are dealing here with what is final and absolute, so that when we speak of the category of leadership, we are on the edge of a precipice, where we can only either hold on to Jesus as the one true Leader or irretrievably go down into the depth. If in this sense we hail Christ as the King of all kings and the Lord of all lords, then the category of *Kyrios* is not merely filled with a new content, but its formal structure undergoes a fundamental change as well. For instead of a leadership that includes only part of our existence, here comes the genuine leadership that encompasses our whole existence, not only the fate of our body but also all our volition and cognition, not only our life until death but our entire future destiny for everlasting. Where there is genuine leadership, there is nothing left in my life that "belongs to myself" that I can keep to myself.

The leadership of Christ is universal because, in contrast to any other leadership we know, it is not concerned with penultimate things, but with the ultimate question which embraces the whole of all that is, the question: does our existence hang on nothing? Or is to exist to stand before God? Is all that we do and suffer a game about vanities, shall we therefore have to get accustomed to the inconceivably difficult thought that the sea of suffering of which human life is full, is meaningless, a suffering to no purpose? Or is there – to put it in the formula of a past time – an ultimate "anchorage" for all that we work and bear, an anchorage which is "the foundation of every life-work", the "guarantee of every plight of troth", "power current from eternity", "pressure from the depths of a world which is more real than our own"?[3]

In this struggle for the ultimate anchorage, the Christian faith declares, we cannot lead ourselves. But we are not left to ourselves. We have been given a Leader. "For unto us a child is born, unto us a son is given, and the government (lordship) shall be upon his shoulder." We may lay our final destiny in His hands. He carries it in His hands. This fact is the centre of the Christian message. The New Testament witnesses to this end and to nothing else.

When Jesus is witnessed to as "the Lord", then there are only two possibilities as regards this testimony. Either it rests on a mistake. Jesus of Nazareth certainly was an important personality, fanatically worshipped by a narrow circle of adherents. But when people attributed to Him world-wide Leader's authority, then this was a dreamer's error which spread like an epidemic and of which many valuable people have become the victims. If Jesus cannot actually lead every present-day man, every German who trusts himself to Him, then we must not treat the illusion which the apostles spread throughout the world with sympathetic neutrality but fight it by all the means at our disposal.

Or the claim of Jesus rests on truth. When we are confronted with Him, we are confronted with our God-given Leader in the ultimate question of life In that case, as Jesus Himself says (Mt. vii.24), we build our whole life, including our political and economic order, on sand if we do not build it on His

[3] Hans Michael Müller, *Glaube und Macht*, Munich 1932, p. 7f.

Leader's word. For in that case the God in whose authority Christ gives us His orders is the only One who can give us that everlasting obligation without which the nation, the army and the civil service fail at the critical moment when they have to make sacrifices for a hopeless cause without any prospect of reward or success.

At the time of Frederick the Great there was still enough left of those ultimate obligations in the Prussian nation for the King to be able, without any danger to the State, calmly to leave everyone to his own convictions and allow him to be saved in his own way. But now, at a time when all the foundations of national morality, e.g. in the field of sexual behaviour, have become largely relative and undermined, it is completely impossible to treat the guidance of man in the ultimate questions of life as a matter of no consequence and to leave this to each person's individualism.

We can of course reject the Apostles' message concerning Christ as a dangerous illusion and form our own opinion of the meaning of life independently of Christ. But if it is true that Christ has received from God the "dominion" over all mankind, then it is only under His leadership that we can acquire a right understanding, not only of the questions of our private life but also of the questions which we have to face as a nation after the catastrophe.

The important thing about the New Testament witness to Christ is therefore not a point of doctrine or a dogmatic or ecclesiastical controversy which the people do not understand, but the quite simple and directly practical question: is what the first Christians said about the universal leadership of the invisible Christ the imagination of ecstatics and fanatics, ignorant of the ways of the world? Or can it be experienced as reality exactly as the leadership of men has always been experienced as an undeniable reality? Under the guidance of Jesus do we really feel that deep calm and certitude and that happiness that releases all our powers, which comes over us when we have placed our whole destiny in the hands of someone who has the royal authority really to lead us?

This question cannot be decided in a scientific way by arguments and counter-arguments, like the truth of a point of doctrine, but can only be verified in practice, on those levels of our life in which everything is at stake, "in the last agony" (*in ultima agone*) as the Reformers used to say. From a theoretical point of view it cannot be discussed at all. For if someone comes forward with a claim of authority which is not limited to our actions but includes our whole existence, then we have to be under his authority in our thinking as well and have to place our cognition under his guidance; or, if we are under another leadership, e.g. under our own, then we must rebel against this claim of authority not only by our actions but also in our reflexion. According to the above-mentioned word of Jesus in the Sermon on the Mount, we must either "love" or "hate" a "Lord" in the full sense of the word; we can only either "hold to" him or "despise" him.

From this follows an important conclusion for the attempt made here reflectingly to develop and describe the content of faith in Christ. If it is true, as the New Testament says, that in grappling with the ultimate questions we have been given a Lord of whom it can truly be said: "Without me you can do nothing," then we cannot even escape from His leadership when reflectingly we develop the content of the Christian faith. For if we are under the guidance of someone then not only our actions but also our thought and cognition are under his guidance. It depends on the leader, whether we can know anything at all about the origin and the aim of the entire course of events, and how much we can know. When an army marches to battle the general can always consider it right to tell his men about only a limited part of the whole plan of campaign. They only need to know the next move. It may happen that the Supreme Command tells the troops only so much about the ultimate reasons and aim of the war as is necessary to prevent them from losing courage and to maintain their belief that they are fighting for a just cause. For the moment it might perhaps not be at all a good thing to tell them more. The leader can tell the men: "I have yet many things to say unto you, but you cannot bear them now." He tells them only so much as they need for the moment. All the rest they can learn later when the suspense is past and the time has come to look back and to think coherently about the experience. Now it is no time to theorise but to hold out and to fight at any risk.

If we lead our lives under the dominion of someone else, then we have also placed our knowledge concerning the ultimate things in his hands. That makes it *a priori* impossible for us for once to direct our attention away from Christ and to form a philosophical or theological conviction about the creation or the order of the world independently of Him and His instruction. We are not permitted to prepare a system of philosophy apart from Him and then afterwards to attribute to Him a place of honour within the total picture so obtained. We are not permitted, as has so often been tried in theology, first to erect a temple of foreign material and then eventually to place Christ as an idol in a niche on a throne of gold. Then we should have left His guidance. At the critical point we should have guided ourselves. If our confession of Him is to be not merely saying "Lord, Lord", if we want to be in earnest about this in practice, then we cannot start without Him when we think about the *original* ground and aim of life and come to Him eventually from some point outside Him. On the contrary His dominion must be the starting point of all our reflexion on the ultimate things. All that we have to say as regards the meaning of the world must start on the one hand from the fact that we need leadership and on the other hand from the fact that He and none other is the Leader.

Any information we can obtain as regards the meaning of the world is therefore not obtainable through our own thoughts about the essence of God and the ordinances of His creation but by beginning from the fact of the dominion of Jesus and then considering what this fact entails for an understanding of the world and of human existence. Our reflexion therefore can at all events merely copy what reality has given us first. If we want to make this attempt, then we first have to take into account the fact that we have been given a Lord, and ask ourselves what this fact means for an understanding of our human situation. Only then can we look at this Lord in his concrete existence and hear what He has to tell us.

CHAPTER 7

*The Element of Truth in the Idealist Belief in the
Possibility of Self-guidance*

IF WE HAVE been given a Lord without whom we "can do
nothing" it follows that we need a Leader if we are to fulfil
our final destiny. For otherwise we would not have been
given a Leader. Why is this necessary? Why can we not reach
the goal by self-guidance? Only Jesus himself can reveal to
us by His words the ultimate ground of this necessity. That will
be discussed in the next section; in this section however we
want to make it clear to ourselves, what kind of answer follows
immediately from the general fact that we have been given a
Leader at all. If, under the influence of the Christian Church,
from our childhood onward we had not heard about our need-
ing a Lord, a Head, a Saviour, an eternal High Priest to find
our right bearings in life, if we were to hear this message for the
first time, then – quite apart from any other objection that can
be raised against this message – we would feel it as a monstrous
demand, as an attack on man's right of self-determination, that
in the decisive question of our life we should surrender the
government to someone else. The Cross is not the first aspect
of the message concerning Christ to scandalise every man. The
offence begins long before we see that contrary to any human
sense of honour and instinct of power the Leader whom we
are to follow allows himself to be executed without resistance
and without being rehabilitated in the eyes of the world.
Certainly the offence of Christianity finds its ultimate and
strongest expression in connexion with this fact. But it begins
long before that. It is already present in the fact that we are
asked to give up our self-determination and to accept the
dominion of Someone else.

It is easy to understand why German Idealism, especially
under the guidance of Fichte, regarded this as an attack on the
most sacred prerogative of the mind. In *Anweisung zum seligen*

Leben Fichte declares: "The peculiar and exclusive standing-point of Christianity, which has only validity for the disciples of that system, looks to the *means* of attaining this True Being, and teaches us thus regarding them: Jesus of Nazareth, absolutely by and through himself, by virtue of his mere existence, nature or instinct, without deliberate act and without guidance or direction, is the perfect sensible manifestation of the Eternal Word, as no one whatever has been before him; while those who become his disciples are, as yet, not so, since they still stand in need of its manifestation in him, but they must first become so through him. This is the characteristic dogma of Christianity, as a phenomenon of Time, as a temporary form of the religious culture of man." Consequently this dogma has no abiding value. In reality "the Eternal Word becomes flesh, assumes a personal, sensible and human existence, without obstruction or reserve, in all times, and in every individual man who has a living insight into his Unity with God, and who actually and in truth gives up his personal life to the Divine Life within him – precisely in the same way as it became incarnate in Jesus Christ." We therefore do not need the mediation of Jesus, even though historically it is "unquestionably true" that we Europeans of today, in virtue of our historical connexion with Christianity, "have done so only through him, and by means of his union with God". "Could Jesus return into the world, we might expect him to be thoroughly satisfied if he found Christianity actually reigning in the minds of men, whether his merit in the work were recognised or overlooked." "If any man be truly united with God, and dwell in him, it is altogether an indifferent thing how he may have reached this state; and it would be a most useless and perverse employment, instead of living in the thing, to be continually repeating over our recollections of the way." That "that German (Luther) who was inspired by the Eternal" still believed that he needed Christ the Mediator for his salvation, that, according to Fichte, is the limitation of his attitude of mind. In this point he had not yet conquered the anguish of soul of the Middle Ages. One must confess "that in the anxiety of that time as regards the salvation of the soul a darkness and lack of clarity remained, because the aim was, not merely to change the external Mediator between God and man but to need no external

Mediator at all and to find the binding connexion within oneself."[1]

German Idealism therefore, of which Fichte is here the spokesman, has either in sharp protest denied that Christ is the Mediator or felt this to be an earth-bound remainder of historical Christianity, with which one has to bear and which one has to understand in its historical context. Fichte's "Philosophy of liberty" is not merely historically relevant. It meets with lively response not only in Germans of the present but in all men of all times. For it is the expression of something universally human. Every unspoilt and unthwarted man instinctively revolts against the attempt to rob him of his independence in the most decisive question of his life. It may be true that in penultimate questions we cannot do without the authority of experts and specialists. But as regards the central question of our existence we want to remain at the helm. Why this is so becomes clear at once, the moment we realise what is actually at stake in this central question of life and how complete our state of dependence becomes if we entrust our destiny to someone else in the search for an answer to this question. For as we saw in the first chapters the question is concerned with the ultimate sanction of our entire life-work and the ultimate Reality to which we can hold even in the most desperate situation. It is very difficult to stomach the fact that at this central point of our existence, in which everything is rooted, we are dependent on outside support. If, because of insufficient training, we cannot find a mathematical formula but have to accept it on the authority of a mathematician, we can bear this dependence because the formula has merely theoretical importance for us. It is already more painful if we are dependent on a medical authority, whose opinion we cannot verify, for a medical diagnosis which is a matter of life and death to us. The more important the question for the solution of which we need outside help, the more painful is this dependence. It must be most painful where everything is at stake for us. Consequently we must rebel with all our soul against the thought that the

---

[1] Fichte, *Anweisung zum seligen Leben*, Lecture VI; the quotations are from W. Smith's translation *The Way towards the blessed Life* (*Popular Works*, VOL. II), London 1848, pp. 388-92; there is a more recent translation by F. Medicus (cf. p. 19, note 13).

Reality compared to which everything else is reduced to utter irrelevance, should not be immediately accessible to us by the mere fact of our existence. The dependence which threatens us here is more thorough and to the natural man, more terrible than any other, e.g. the dependence of a worker on his employer or that of a slave on his lord.

The great positive importance of German Idealism for the question concerning God is that it has expressed the burning desire of every man to be dependent on no one and to determine his own destiny in the central question of his life. That would be possible if the reality which is the ultimate sanction of our actions and the anchorage of our faith were immediately disclosed together with our mere existence, in other words if Schleiermacher were right in declaring: We can say that God-consciousness has been given to us together with our consciousness as part of our self-consciousness.[2] If this were so, then the way to the Absolute would be immediately open to me within the given world. By my mere existence and my finding myself as the centre of the universe, access to God would be open to me, not merely as a question waiting for an answer but as a question already answered. I would find that I am in God exactly in the same way as I find that I am a spatial being in three dimensions. Wherever I may go or be, in the dim kitchen of a basement flat or on the snowy top of a mountain with wide views across blue lakes and glaciers, the third dimension is open to me not merely as a direction from which something could be received, but as always full of an extremely rich, inexhaustible content. I just have to take my choice. Idealism believes that in exactly the same way the knowledge of God's essence and will is part of my self-consciousness. I merely have to sink into the depths of myself, and I am in God. At least that is how it should be. But this burning desire cannot be fulfilled. Idealism awakens in us the memory of paradise lost, where, as we may well suspect, we were destined to be but from which we are now excluded. Idealism is like the song of home that Blondel sings outside the prison

---

[2] Friedrich Schleiermacher, *Der christliche Glaube* (usually cited as *Glaubenslehre*), Reutlingen 1822 and many revised editions since; Engl. trans. of 2nd German edn. *The Christian Faith*, by H. R. Mackintosh, J. S. Stewart *et al.*, Edinburgh 1928, p. 17.

of Richard Coeur de Lion to call the king to the barred window
of his cell. It merely deepens the king's consciousness of being
far from his country, languishing in captivity.

CHAPTER 8

The Breaking down of Idealism on Reality

WE CANNOT find out for ourselves why we have been expelled from our homeland, why the idealist interpretation of our situation is an ideal picture in contrast with actual fact. Only He, who alone has the authority to solve the riddle of human existence, can answer this question for us. But that the Absolute is not so open to us as it should be according to the idealist hypothesis is a fact that we can bring home to anyone in whom the question concerning God has been aroused. We only have to realise what human life would be like if the consciousness of God really were part of our self-consciousness and compare our actual situation with that.

If we assume that the Reality of realities is immediately accessible to us as, when we look at a landscape, the third dimension is open to us with its entire space and content, then there could not arise any doubt concerning God, any irreligious propaganda, any atheism; indeed no one could even conceive of the idea of thinking of a proof for the existence of God, just as it does not occur to us to prove our own existence. To doubt the reality of God would be just as inconceivable as to doubt the existence of a scene that arises before me. Even if it were possible to prove beyond doubt the existence of God, yet the fact that it occurs to us even to think of such a demonstration shows that we are in a condition of being far from God. Think what that means: the absolute Reality before which any other reality is irrelevant, the *original* Being to which all that is owes its reality, is so hidden, that the question can arise, whether it exists at all. The existential power of the *original* Reality is continually put in the shade by the obtrusive visibility and conspicuousness, which charms and intoxicates our senses, of those things and beings which all have a merely second-hand existence because they have only borrowed their being from God's *original* Being and have only a shadowy existence beside Him.

The created world therefore has pushed aside, covered up and put in the shade the *original* Reality by which it lives from moment to moment. This is the contradictory situation that confronts with a riddle everyone who is convinced of the reality of God. This riddle becomes even more difficult if we realise the consequences which follow from the mysteriousness of God.

If, as Idealism believes, by our mere existence the Absolute were accessible to us, then the other beings to whom we can have an "I-thou" relationship should also be immediately open to us. For then everyone else, exactly like I myself, would with his being rest immediately in God and have in Him his immovable centre of gravity. We then would be mutually open to each other in the centre of our being. Everyone would immediately know what the other regards as the only real value and where the "eternal magnet" is by which alone he is attracted. That we can be strangers to one another, that it can happen at all that I do not understand someone else and do not know what he wants, is a sign that God is not open to us. Our "being far from the neighbour" is merely the result of our being far from God. But our being far from the neighbour is the reason of all the tragic misunderstandings between "I" and "thou", the reason of the roughness and cruelty with which we wound and ill-treat each other in the pitiless struggle of life. If everyone knew what the other's innermost being is like, then we should not be able to do that at all.

Beside this there is a second detail that shows our godless condition. If by our very existence God were already open to us, then we should not only at any given moment be certain of God but also act according to God. For all that happens comes from God, the *original* Source of being. There can be no checking of the Absolute. He cannot meet with resistance. For everything has been determined by Him. Therefore all that happens can only have one direction. Our actions should be part of the proceeding that comes forth from the *Origin*. We should act as people full of God (ἔνθεοι), as organs and instruments of the Absolute. Then we should have no choice as to whether or not our actions were in harmony with the Absolute. For there would be no question of anything else. Consequently no hesitation, no faltering would be possible. Our will would be completely full of one purpose. We should have an absolute relation to the Absolute.

Fichte is perfectly right when he describes the normal condition: "The Religious Man is forever secured from the possibility of Doubt and Uncertainty. In every moment he knows distinctly what he wills, and ought to will; for the innermost root of his Life – his Will – for ever flows forth from the Divinity, immediately and without the possibility of error; its indication is infallible, and for that indication he has an infallible perception. In every moment he knows assuredly that in all Eternity he shall know what he shall will, and ought to will; that in all Eternity the fountain of Divine Love which has burst forth in him shall never be dried up, but shall uphold him securely, and bear him onward for ever. It is the root of his Existence; it has now risen upon him clear and bright, and his eye is fixed upon it with unspeakable Love: how could that fountain ever be dried up, how could that leader and guardian ever turn aside?"[1] That we are in a godless condition therefore is not merely shown by the fact that we do not with all our heart do what appears to us to be God's will and that we do not devote ourselves to it with a pure heart and an undivided will. No, it is already abnormal that we do not as a matter of course know what God wants of us at this particular moment, that it is not self-evident what the absolutely right thing is in this particular situation. It is an indication of our being far from God that the question what we have to do arises at all, that a decision in favour of God's will is necessary at all. For a decision always presupposes that we are standing at the crossroads, that there is another possibility as well and that we are conscious of our ability to act differently.

The question what we are to do is a sign of that indecision of which Shakespeare has given such a staggering picture in the figure of Hamlet. This Hamlet-fate which continually checks our actions and prevents us from taking sure and confident steps is something universally human. It is true that there are cases in which what is to be done follows immediately from the situation. Our country is attacked by enemies: we hurry to take up our arms, to safeguard hearth and home. A child has fallen over in the middle of a busy thoroughfare: we jump into

[1] Fichte, *Way towards the blessed Life*, trans. Smith, lecture X, pp. 483-4.

F

the road to pick it up. At night we see a house on fire: we run to the fire-alarm box. But such cases in which we are relieved of the burden of reflexion as to what we are to do, in which there is only one possible course in which we have to do our utmost, are not the rule in our life but very rare exceptions. This is shown by the fact that in spite of the agitation and the mortal danger usually involved we always experience these cases as a great relief.

In 1914 countless people who did not know what to do with their lives and therefore suffered with depressive psychological conditions were cured at once. Mobilisation had called them to the barracks and placed them under an authority which told them every hour what they had to do. The heavy mountain of unsolved questions as to how to spend the next hour had gone. They could breathe freely again. In such cases, in the midst of extreme distress and agitation, we experience something of the *original* state of man which in an entirely different form also comes to poets and artists in the great moments of inspiration. This is the *original* condition in which as yet there is no choice, in which we are in a situation as yet prior to any decision.

These cases in which so to speak in a clairvoyant certitude we move on the narrow ridge between two precipices are extraordinarily rare. They generally occur only at highly dramatic moments of history, at moments of fate. As soon as things are calm again and we have returned to normal conditions the old indecision comes over us again, the anxiety whether we are on the right way, whether what we do is not altogether wrong, the uncertain feeling of walking in the mist. That this Hamlet-like indecision is our usual condition is the only reason why we men have a need which the animal with its sure instinct does not seem to know, viz. a need of ethics, of laws, commandments, ordinances, norms, formulation of values, ideals, examples, in short of something that illuminates and prescribes at least part of the way into the dark future.

This need would never have arisen if we were able to remain in the *original* state which we experience in those rare moments of action without choice. Therefore the very need of ethics is already something abnormal, a lapse compared with what we surmised as a remote possibility in those great hours. That is also why all that is done to satisfy this need is always an emergency measure or an insufficient substitute for what we really need, viz. the inspiration of the moment. No ethics or casuistry, however specialised, can ever really set me free of the burden of uncertainty as to what I am to do this minute. The whole history of conflicts of conscience and any guidance of conscience in the confessional will bear that out.

Why is this impossible? No situation in which I have to act is really in every detail like any previous situation any more than a leaf of a tree is exactly the same as another leaf or a shell washed up on the shore by the sea is precisely the same as another shell. Every situation is new in relation to all previous situations. Therefore it has no real precedent. A rule can only combine a number of cases in a more or less similar situation and indicate a general direction in which one should move in such cases. But even the most circumspect casuistry cannot set me free from the uncertainty as to whether I really have done right, because every situation is new.

In Jer. xxxi.33-4 a new Covenant between God and the people is promised in which any moral and religious instruction will become obsolete. "I will put my law within them, and I will write it upon their hearts . . . and no longer shall each man teach his neighbour and each his brother, saying, 'Know the Lord', for they shall all know me, from the least of them to the greatest." Measured by the new condition in which the destiny of man will finally be fulfilled every code of ethics, every law which man receives from without through someone else, however perfect it may be, always appears to be something inferior, an indication of our being far from God, a merely provisional and insufficient substitute for the immediate guidance under which we should actually be. The invisible wall that separates us from God therefore becomes noticeable not only because we transgress against the commandment and are incapable of fulfilling it; no, indeed the very fact that we need a commandment at all is already abnormal.

In his Lectures on the Epistle to the Romans of 1515-16[2] Luther stated that the imperative mood in which the will of the Absolute confronts us is already impure. It should not be

---

[2] Clemen, VOL. V; Johannes Ficker, *Anfänge reformatorischer Bibelauslegung*, 2nd edn., VOL. I, Leipzig 1923.

a "must", a commandment that faces us with a decision. That which is our destiny should not come as a command from without but should entirely fill our innermost being. That I am told from without what I must do is only because I am not immediately absolutely sure of my destiny. That signposts have to be erected to show me the direction is only because I am continually in danger of losing my way. If I had a reliable compass in myself, it would not occur to me to look up to the stars to find my bearing. But I am in the abnormal condition which Fichte means when he says: "Unblessedness comes of Doubt which continually drags us to and fro, and of Uncertainty which spreads around us an impenetrable night in which our feet can find no sure path."[3]

Something else too is connected with this indecision as regards what is the right thing at this particular moment, viz. the weakness of will and the lack of energy which prevent us from applying and carrying through our will as we should. As soon as the paralysing doubt in respect of the vanity of my resolution has disappeared completely, as soon as I know with all my heart, "God wills it", then unlimited power to fulfil the lofty task pervades me. I live by the Absolute. The belief awakes in me that nothing can resist the Power under whose orders I am. When the disciples were amazed that the fig-tree had withered at the command of Jesus, He spoke the unbeliev-able words: "Truly, I say to you, whoever says to this moun-tain, 'Be taken up and cast into the sea,' and does not doubt in his heart, but believes that what he says will come to pass, it will be done for him" (Mk. xi.23).

When the disciples could not cast out the demon, Jesus certainly did not admit that there are extremely difficult cases of illness which confront any human help with insuperable limits, before which we have to submit to the inevitable. According to the word of Jesus the defeat of the disciples had only one reason. To the question: "Why could not we cast it out?" Jesus replies: "Because of your little faith, for truly, I say to you, if you have faith as a grain of mustard seed, you will say to this mountain, 'Move hence to yonder place', and it will move; and nothing will be impossible to you" (Mt. xvii.20). Jesus therefore is convinced that the only thing that

[3] Fichte, *Way towards the blessed Life*, trans. Smith, p. 483.

prevents us from overcoming all the obstacles in the way of our will, and from doing unheard-of works of power is "doubting in our hearts", the trembling incertitude as to whether what we want to do really is the right thing. As soon as incertitude left us, as soon as we knew with absolute certainty that God really wills that which we want to do, nothing would be impossible to us. For then we should live immediately by the *Origin* from which all things have come. We should therefore share immediately in the infinite current of energy from which not only we ourselves but all the natural forms around us are continually derived. That we are weak and so often fail over obstacles is caused by our being far from God, which prevents us from taking sure steps.

This brings us to a further consequence of our godless situation, the suffering by which our life is accompanied. Schleiermacher in his *Glaubenslehre*,[4] introducing the doctrine of evil, says of the contrast between world and man: "As long as every moment of human activity might have been a product of the original perfection of man, every moment being determined by the God-consciousness, and all the sensuous and bodily aspects of life being brought into an exclusive relation to it, that opposition could never have been construed by the corporate consciousness as an obstruction to life, since it could not in any sense act as an inhibition of the God-consciousness, but at most would give a different form to its effects. This holds good even of natural death and the bodily afflictions that precede it in the shape of disease and debility: for what can no longer serve the guiding and determining higher consciousness, is not willed." This thesis contains an important truth from which we have to start if we want to understand what suffering is and what is the actual reason of our suffering.

Suffering or pain is not an objective phenomenon that can be observed and measured as a natural phenomenon – e.g. a chemical reaction or an electric discharge – can be observed and measured. If we were able objectively to observe the course of the world without ourselves being involved, then we would not notice anything of the pain and suffering in the world, not even in a medieval torture-chamber or on a battlefield covered with groaning wounded soldiers. That people are

[4] *The Christian Faith*, pp. 315-16.

suffering in such places is something that we do not know through objective observation. We know this only through ourselves, viz. because the distorted faces and heart-rending cries remind us of moments in our own lives in which we made similar movements and gave out similar sounds. For pain is something that we can never place objectively before us, but that has its place within ourselves. It is what happens when my will meets with resistance and collides with something else that restrains my vitality and keeps it down. According to the dynamic view of the world that we advocate, the other thing that pains and hurts me cannot possibly be a dead object, something that has already come to be (*etwas schon Gewordenes*). It must be something living, viz. the becoming (*das Werden*) of an object that comes into conflict with that becoming in which I participate by my own existence. Even if I suffer in a condition, which, as people usually say, always remains the same, e.g. a chain that binds me to a rock or a prison wall that bars my way out of the narrow cell, even then what makes me suffer is, strictly speaking, not the chain or the wall as an object. That against which I rebel is the invisible power that regardless of my protest from moment to moment maintains and renews those fettering objects. I rattle my chains. I run my head against the wall. But that other thing against which I fight is stronger than I am. Over and over again it lends to the iron rings and the stone masonry the power to resist my pulling and pushing so that in ever renewed impotent rage I have to yield. Pain is what happens when a vehement, fruitless struggle is fought between my will to live and the power that wants to suffocate it. That applies in exactly the same way to mental pain, as for example, sorrow at the ruin of one's country, as it does to physical pain like rheumatism or toothache.

If pain always originates from our fighting a restraining power, on what then does the strength of the pain depend? Not on the event as such that restrains our will to live but on the relation between this event and our will. The deeper the conflict, the greater the pain. Consequently the pain would be reduced to zero if I could manage to give up my resistance to the restraining power.

This fact brings us back to our starting point, the religious import of the experience of suffering, expressed in Schleiermacher's thesis. If God is real, then, as we saw, He is the Creator, the *Origin* of all that happens. As his creature I should in my will be one with that which God wills. My will should offer no resistance to what happens to me. For it all comes from God. If, as Schleiermacher says, every moment of my life were "determined by the God-consciousness, and all the sensuous and bodily aspects of life being brought into an exclusive relation to it", then no event could "have been construed by the corporate consciousness as an obstruction to life" and therefore cause suffering. Together with resistance to restraint, pain would be eliminated as well.

In spite of all their differences all the higher religions and philosophies have expressed this thought in remarkable concord. Buddhism is an effort to soothe pain by lowering as much as possible the flame of the will to live. For it is the will to live that causes pain by its resistance to destructive power. One endeavours to approach the state of a dead man whose will to live has been extinguished so that it no longer reacts to any incentive, and has thus become immune to pain. From totally different presuppositions Fichte arrives at the same thought: "To the religious man," he declares, "whatever comes to pass around him, nothing appears to him strange or unaccountable; – he knows assuredly, whether he understand it or not, that it is in God's World, and that there nothing can be that does not directly tend to Good. . . . He has never aught to deny himself, nor aught to long for; for he is at all times in eternal possession of the fulness of all that he is capable of enjoying. For him all labour and effort have vanished; his whole Outward Ex-istence flows forth, softly and gently, from his Inward Being, and issues out into Reality without difficulty or hindrance."[5] Luther too, who starts from entirely different presuppositions from Fichte's, has stated: If I really do love God with all my heart and consequently will only that which God wills, then God may send me to hell and I shall yet be blessed in the midst of hell. My unblessedness is caused only because my will is not in tune with God's will, because I still aspire to my own happiness and consequently do not simply will what God wills.

If what is stated in remarkable concord by entirely different philosophies is true, then it follows that the very fact that we

[5] *Way towards the blessed Life*, trans. Smith, p. 484.

suffer at all, that there is pain of any kind in the world, is a sign that we are not so near to God and that we do not live so exclusively by Him as we ought according to the idealist axiom. With every misfortune we experience, the more we approach the attitude of accepting with all our heart even an unbearable fate and "do not wish for anything else",[6] the more bearable everything becomes and the more we approach the original relationship to God from which we have fallen. We never really reach that state. This shows us our godless condition.

This brings us to the last fact which shows us that we live in a state of being far from God. That is our invincible horror of death. The manner in which we approach death is conclusive evidence as to whether being-in-God is accessible to us immediately by the fact of our existence. If God-consciousness belongs to our self-consciousness, then it is of no interest to us what death actually is and what it does to the form in which we have so far existed. The being-in-God, that by our mere existence is ours even now, cannot be destroyed by anything we may still have before us. For it is participation in God's eternity. "In every moment to be eternal is the immortality of religion."[7] Because we cannot be robbed of this eternity, anything else that may happen to us in death can be of no consequence to us. There is not the slightest reason to be afraid of death. What is there actually to fear? Terror of death should be simply incomprehensible to us.

But what is the situation in reality? All the views and theories which men have invented about death and what follows originate in the need to dispel the terror which seizes us when we are confronted with the unknown X that approaches us in death, to banish the fear caused by this event that comes nearer and nearer and that we cannot comprehend. The sedative of materialism is the most simple. Consciousness must fade out with the decay of the material brain, just as the lamp goes out when there is no oil left. Consequently what we have before us is precisely what thousands of people these days wish for themselves: *lethe*, dreamless sleep. But as soon as a convinced

[6] Johann Müller.

[7] Schleiermacher, *Ueber die Religion, Reden an die Gebildeten unter ihren Verächtern*, 2nd edn., Berlin 1806, p. 177; Engl. trans. *On Religion, Speeches to its cultured Despisers*, by J. Oman, London 1893, p. 101. Cf. H. R. Mackintosh, *Types of Modern Theology*, London 1937, p. 55.

materialist desires to take his own life to liberate himself from the painful memories that haunt him, then he notices distinctly how uncertain this whole calculation is. That our consciousness becomes extinct, is merely a conclusion from the outward picture of death that we receive when we see others die. But what the dying man himself experiences remains entirely unknown to us. For we cannot look into him. The materialistic interpretation of death therefore is merely a sedative used by man, which betrays his fear of death.

What we have said about the negative sedative of materialism is equally true of the positive efforts that have been made to banish the fear of destruction. Particularly calming seems the following idea, of Indian origin: in death I surrender only my individual existence, which in any case is very often a burden to me, and return to Universal Life to continue in it. We Europeans are more familiar with the Platonic concept of immortality. In death only the perishable tent of the body, the prison of the soul is destroyed: nothing at all happens to me: I remain what I am, and am only transferred to higher regions. One can see at once that these theories concerning the essence of death have been invented only for the practical purpose of providing us with a good idea in the face of death, which is to make dying easier for us by delivering us from the fear of destruction. This aim is reached only very imperfectly. Even if we entirely disregard the objections which present-day psychology and brain-pathology raise against the idea of a bodiless spirit, everyone who has once, in a time of serious illness, experienced the approach of death, knows by experience that death does not merely break the outer shell of our human being to set free the imperishable centre; indeed, death attacks our inner self, the centre of our personality.

Therefore despite all men's negative and positive conceptions of death, in death's presence we remain in uncertainty, as pictured in Hamlet's monologue: "To be, or not to be, that is the question." We are thrown to and fro between those two possibilities. Does one pass through death into nothingness? Into a "sleep"? Or is there beyond this *nothing* an unknown *something*: "perchance to dream"?

This uncertainty is not in itself a sign that we live in a condition of being far from God; but the terror with which this uncertainty fills us is. If we were in God as we are in space, if God's presence were as open to us as the dimensions of space are, then the uncertain destiny which awaits us in death need not make any impression on us at all. For the eternity which we have in God is completely independent of all that can happen to the perishable part of our being. That by nature we are all afraid of death, shows that there is something between God and us. By all kinds of means we can deaden and suppress that fear of death. We do become more serene, if in hours of mortal danger we read Plato's *Phaedo* and bring to our mind the death of Socrates. The fear of death can be kept down especially by activity, by participation in a great action which claims all our strength. "Everyone who has taken part in the war or in great dangers knows that in the intensified moments of nearness of death a delirious levity can prevail which robs the world of its reality and therefore eliminates fear."[8] But the way in which in all those cases we can overcome the fear of death shows clearly that fearlessness in the face of death is never found with us men by nature, but that we can only reach it by repressing our natural state to the subconscious level. Apart from these cases our original condition can be described by what the Epistle to the Hebrews says of man in the pre-Christian stage: that "through fear of death" they "were subject to lifelong bondage" (Heb. 11.15).

If we look back once more, a whole series of characteristic features has appeared, which stamps our existence as a being far from God: the obscurity of God, i.e. the possibility of doubting the Reality which underlies all things, our being far from our neighbour, the uncertainty of our decisions and therefore the need of ethical norms, this insufficient substitute for the inspiration of the moment, the weakness of our will connected with this uncertainty, the suffering of life and the terror of death. All these are indications that we are not in the state which Idealism correctly describes as the normal state of man. They are all facts which remind every man in whom the question concerning God has been awakened, that God is not open to us by the mere fact of our existence so that we can lead ourselves in the central question of life. From this we see that if there is to be any possibility of our finding God, this can

[8] Franz Werfel.

happen only in one way, a way against which not only Aryan man but every man by nature rebels with all his strength, viz. by giving up our self-determination in the most important question of our life and allowing ourselves to be led by someone else who has the authority to do so.

What is the origin of this abnormal situation from which we can be liberated only by such extraordinary means? By our own thinking we cannot give an answer to this question. For as long as we are blind to God we cannot penetrate the cause of this blindness. For if we could know the cause of our abnormal condition then there would at least be the possibility of liberating ourselves from it. Then we would not really be blind to God. Consequently we can recognise the deepest reason for our blindness only if we submit to Him who has the authority to lead us in the ultimate question of life.

But we cannot speak about the real reason for our abnormal state before the next chapter. For there we shall first pay attention to the Leader himself in His concrete reality and hear what He has told us about that and what has been made manifest by His whole attitude to the world. We have so far merely realised what is entailed by the fact that we have been given a Leader at all.

PART THREE

ORIGINAL SIN AS THE DEEPEST REASON WHY WE NEED A LEADER

CHAPTER 9

Satanic Power in Jesus' view of the World

IN THE first sections, which formed the negative preparation for the early Christian confession of faith, we have endeavoured to make it clear to ourselves that the *original* Reality which alone can give us an unshakeable foundation of life is outside the reach of our human knowledge. It is suprapolar; all our cognition, imagination and thought moves within polar relations. Consequently our cognition can make only two movements. Either we fix an initial point of the series and make this into an idol of our own making; or we return to the state of indifference. Neither movement leads beyond the polar relations. In the last section we have discussed the idealist belief in the possibility of self-guidance, and demonstrated by the simple facts of everyday life that the ultimate Reality that supports us is not accessible to us like our own existence or the dimensions of space. We live in a condition of being far from God.

Both belong together: the blindness-to-God of our cognitive powers and the practical experience of our being far from God. These are merely two sides of the same thing. So far we have only stated that the limitation of our cognition and the experience of our being far from God are facts that show us that we cannot lead ourselves. These facts are so abnormal, that we are inescapably faced with the question why that is so. This question arises in its entire urgency as soon as we are in God's presence. We cannot ourselves bring about the impression that God is near. Only God himself can force upon us the impression of His immediate presence. Whether and how He desires to do this is His concern. But as soon as we are impressed with the presence of God and have but the merest notion of the calm that comes over us when we are in God's hand, we get alarmed at our godless condition and ask: how is it possible that we, to whom such great things are open, live in blindness to God and far from Him?

The question acquires a very definite colour because it is asked in the presence of God. For the very moment we enter into God's presence, a new category comes into being, which would not exist if there were not an ultimate absolute Reality, viz. the category of the ethical, the duty of highest responsibility. As soon as this category exists, the question arises: is the condition of being far from God, in which we live, something for which we are not responsible, a destiny, a fatality, a situation in which we find ourselves? Or is this condition our fault? Are we responsible for being in this condition?

Before we attempt to find an answer to this question we have to make it clear to ourselves, why the question is so pointed. It is Kant's lasting contribution to ethics that he has shown us that the ethical is not discovered as a category by itself and made free of any intermixture with the pleasurable, the beautiful and the efficient, that there cannot be any guilt and responsibility proper unless there is a commandment that has absolute validity, that bears a sanction which is in need of no higher sanction, an authority which needs no superior court to confirm it. If there is no source of absolute authority, if therefore the question concerning the rightness of our human actions leads to an endless series, then the question what is good or bad can be decided only by our setting up or choosing something, the legitimacy of which we no longer desire to question, a measure which we ourselves fix as an ultimate criterion. This measure, which we choose for ourselves, can be either that which makes us happy, or that which we find beautiful, or that which has success in the world and therefore bewitches us. But that does not yet produce the category of the ethical. As Kant says, all maxims and principles to which we conform may be merely counsels of shrewdness or technical rules which we have adopted or arranged because of our own or other people's experience.

Such principles do not differ in any respect from hygienic advice and rules of conduct given by the physician to tell us how to guard against a cold, or from the rules which a technician or an engineer has to take into account if he wants to construct a durable building or a safe mountain suspension railway. They do not try to place me under an absolute obligation. They just say: if you want to remain in good health, then follow the advice of the physician; if you want to ruin your health, just take no notice of the advice. If you want to build a mountain railway which is safe against accidents, then use the best materials and make use of the experience gained from the building of the most recent suspension railways; but if the safety of the passengers means nothing to you, you can also build with inferior material according to an antiquated system. Counsels of prudence and technical advice give me no answer to the question whether I ought to preserve or ruin my health, whether I aught to give preference to the safety of the public or to economy. None of them contain an absolute commandment. They are therefore all outside the ethical field.

They do not attain to the category of the ethical. Certainly, if we like, we can widen the idea of ethics to include all that can be the object of a sense of value. But as long as we want to distinguish the ethical as a particular field from other spheres of value, as long as we want to distinguish between what is the duty of conscience and what is merely pleasant, merely a matter of taste or fashion, we must say that a principle, a value, an instinct, an exemplary man is ethical only if it or he imposes on me an absolute responsibility which does not consult my wishes but holds good under any circumstances and does not depend on any condition. Consequently one can speak of ethics in the proper sense of the word only if there is an authority which in itself has the right to command us. This final authority, which itself needs no legitimation but by which every command must be authorised if it is to have absolute validity, we call God.

If we have understood that God is the *original* Reality, then in all that we think and do we stand before Him to whom we owe ourselves entirely and to whom therefore we are absolutely responsible. Consequently the question arises, whether all that happens around us and in us is a vicissitude of fate for which we have no responsibility at all because it is outside our control, or whether we are responsible for it to God. This question becomes most urgent, when in the presence of God we realise that we are living far from Him and therefore are capable of doubting God, of weakness, indecision and fear of death. Is this condition fate or guilt? Am I innocent or am I responsible for it? That is the either-or with which we are faced.

G

Everything depends for us on the decision as regards this either-or. As compared to this main question any other questions which we can still ask become minor side-issues. If we can accept our condition of being far from God as a vicissitude of fate for which we have no responsibility, then the next question is merely of theoretical importance to us: how we are philosophically and theologically to interpret this fate to which we are subjected and how we shall express it philosophically. We can say: our blindness to God, our suffering and our indecision simply belong to our human condition. For our spirit is imprisoned in a material body that weighs it down like a heavy ballast and checks its eagle's flight up to God. Or we can say: our soul has not only reason but also sensuality, which intoxicates it and pulls it down to a position of being far from God. Or we can understand our condition in the Brahmin way: we are enveloped by the veil of Māyā which makes us believe that we are individual beings who have to maintain themselves by mutual greed and hatred, while really we are at one with Atma and Brahma. Or we can describe our situation in the form of German speculative philosophy and say that it is our destiny to participate in a world-process developing along dialectical lines: an affirmation can come about only by the negation of a negation. The spirit has to be estranged from itself to find itself.   •

All these heterogeneous interpretations of our abnormal state are only variations on a single theme. They can all be understood as various forms of the words with which in the biblical story of the Fall man excused himself before God: "The woman whom thou gavest to be with me, she gave me fruit of the tree, and I ate" (Gen. III.12). We can vary these words: the physical body which thou gavest me has estranged me from Thee and my being far from Thee is due to that. The sensuality which Thou hast added to my reason gave me from the forbidden tree and I ate. The delusion of my individual existence has blinded me and I have lost unity with the universal Being. The dialectic tension of the world-process from which Thou hast caused me to arise contains as an inevitable antithesis estrangement from Thee.

Our situation is entirely different and we are driven out of all these philosophical and theological considerations and placed on an entirely different level, if our severance from our origin is not a fate to be borne courageously or resignedly, but a guilt of which we have to give an account.

How then is the question to be answered, whether this is a case of destiny or a case of guilt? We cannot ourselves decide on this question. For God is out of reach of our polar perception, imagination and thought. He can never become the object of our thinking. Neither can we therefore make the relation between God and our existence an object of reflexion and examine its origin and cause. If we try to do so we go beyond the limitation set to us. Therefore there are only two possibilities left: either we resolutely abandon all efforts to reach any further with our reflexion. Or there is a power that takes the lead in all our reflexion and volition, when we can no longer guide ourselves. According to the belief of the Church of Christ we have been given a Leader who reveals as much concerning our relationship to God as He finds proper so that we shall not go wrong. According to the record of the Gospels the first disciples, when they could not find an answer to a vital question, surrounded their Master and put the question before Him, e.g. "When is the Kingdom of God coming?" In this sense we ask Jesus the question: Why are we so far from God, from that God who is nearer to us than we are to ourselves? Is this a fate that we have to accept or is it guilt?

Nowhere has Jesus given a direct answer to this question. But His decision is shown by His whole understanding of His task in life. In that respect He is clearly distinguished from Buddha and other leaders of Indian religion. Unlike Buddha Jesus did not wish to show people a way out of suffering, an island where one could save oneself from the ocean of the suffering of the world. He did not come as the leader of a rescue party to an area hit by a serious disaster, e.g. a crop failure or a famine. Jesus does not fight against a fate that has befallen man. He fights against a will that has rebelled against God. After the Spirit had come upon Him in His baptism, He started His life's work by taking up the fight with Satan. Satan tried to quench the fire that Jesus was to light upon earth before it could spread. The devil wished to tempt Him to inspire the masses by miraculous powers and mighty deeds and to aim at mass-results. That would have brought about a movement of earthly power which would soon have broken down. In violent struggle Jesus crushes the enemy. Luke concludes his report with these words: "And when the devil had ended every temptation he departed from him until an opportune time "(iv.13). The story of the temptation therefore is merely the first battle in a prolonged war. The whole life of Jesus is a war with God's mortal enemy. The aim of this war is to enter into the "strong man's house", to overpower him, to bind him and to take his spoil away (Mk. iii.27).

Satan knows that there has come upon the scene One stronger than himself, who is to make an end of his dominion. He consequently offers resistance with every arm at his disposal. No sooner has Jesus the sower begun to sow the seed than "Satan immediately comes and takes away the word which is sown in them" (Mk. iv.15). Whenever Jesus wants to help men the demons rebel against Him. In the bent-down woman Jesus sees a prisoner-of-war of Satan. "For eighteen years" he has bound "a daughter of Abraham", i.e. someone who shared in God's promise (Lk. xiii.16). Nearer and nearer comes the terrible hour when the enemy will proceed to the final blow and rally all his forces to challenge Jesus to the decisive battle. The enemy even enters into the most intimate circle of the disciples: "Satan demanded to have you, that he might sift you like wheat," Jesus says to his disciples (Lk. xxii.31). Satan took possession of Judas: "Then after the morsel, Satan entered into him" (Jn. xiii.27). And as now the hour had come when the leaders of Israel had managed to enlist the military power of Rome against Him and Jesus was surrounded by the temple-guard led by the priests and elders, He spoke the significant words: "This is your hour, and the power of darkness" (Lk. xxii.53).

The mortal suffering which He faces is therefore not vocational suffering caused by human misunderstanding and resistance. Neither is it a struggle between ideas, e.g. between a national-political and a purely religious concept of the Messiah. On the contrary, according to Jesus' own assertion it is the final battle, terrible and decisive, of the war that fills the whole of His life, against the satanic power that wants to dethrone God. This state of affairs, which is unanimously recorded by all the sources of the life of Jesus, is in itself sufficient to show that the thought of an anti-godly power against which this war is waged cannot be eliminated from the mind of Jesus as an unimportant concept to be attributed to popular ideas of His time. On the contrary: this is the fundamental conviction that makes His whole life-work from the beginning to the terrible end into a fierce war with an invisible enemy. The agony in Gethsemane and all that follows can be understood only in this light.

What are the consequences as regards our question? Regarded merely from the point of view of comparative religion it is extraordinary that in a religion which is entirely full of and dominated by the belief in a single God, the Father who clothes the lilies and feeds the birds, there should be room at all for the dark concept of a satanic power. In polydemonistic religion it is an obvious thought, that the world is populated not only by deities of light but also by dark demons who frighten men by their diabolical tricks. But should not this whole devil's work be finished the moment that the belief in one God as represented by Moses rises victoriously like the sun above the mist of pagan concepts of demons? "Hear O Israel: the Lord our God is one Lord." "The Lord is God and no one other." "You shall have no other gods beside me (before me, R.S.V.)."

What does it mean if the word "Satan" appears in the context of a view of the world that is entirely dominated by the belief in the one Creator of heaven and earth? Is this a lapse into the obsolete religious state of polytheism, a stain on the pure picture of Jesus' belief in the Father? That would be an incomprehensible inconsistency as far as Jesus is concerned, for whom belief in the sole authority of God dominates everything. Moreover we ought to realise that the reality of Satan has a central place in Jesus' view of life. It is essential to the way in which He understands His task as a Saviour. If we reject this as a concept due to the ideas of His time, i.e. deny its truth because we regard it as a subjective error, then we destroy Jesus' whole authority over us as a Leader in the ultimate question.

CHAPTER 10

The Essence of the Satanic

WHAT DOES it mean, that He, who knew that all that happens happens according to the will of the Father and that not a hair of our head falls without Him, has reckoned with the reality of Satan? When one speaks of diabolical power, then at any event three things are meant:

1. What brings about a disturbance in the relationship between Creator and creature is not an impersonal power, not a defect, a weakness, an imperfection belonging to the destiny of our finite world but a will. The satanic is not a negation but something very positive. Satan is a hostile will that rebels against God.

2. In addition a second thing is immediately implicit as soon as the word "Satan" is mentioned. The will that rebels against God is not a limited human will, for whose rebellion there is some kind of explanation or excuse. If a weak human will rebels against God the reason behind it may be a lack of knowledge of God. Man does not understand God's guidance and for that reason cannot overcome his doubt concerning God, however much he may try. Or the human will is too weak to resist the temptations which lure it away from God. The world is so beautiful and bewitching that man yields to temptation. In all these cases the struggle with God always has some reason which is not to be found in God's essence. Rebellion against God can be explained by a misunderstanding of God or by the bewitching power of the world that holds us fast. But with the satanic will against God the case is entirely different: it has no reason or excuse either in weakness or in lack of knowledge. This is hatred of God *tout court*. The devil knows who God is and what He wants. And he hates precisely this God in His divine majesty with all his soul. He wishes to destroy precisely this God. "We do not want this man to reign over us" (Lk. XIX.14).

3. But the third is the most important. A will that wills God's destruction cannot be a power which is merely another point in the series of objects, spaces and factors which mutually qualify and limit each other. For God as the *original* Reality is beyond and above all the polar contrasts of the empirical world. That is the only reason why leaning on Him we can defy the whole world. It is inconceivable that an energy which itself is polar and limited should rebel against the omnipresent supra-polar Reality. A power which wishes to wage total war against God thereby presumes to take God's place. It wishes to dethrone God and itself to be god. In this sense Satan is called in the New Testament the "god of this world" (II Cor. IV.4).

These statements confront us with an abysmal, difficult and inconceivable truth. If we attempt to think it out, a host of questions rushes upon us. How can an opposing power rise against God within His Realm? What about the sole dominion of God? Does this not cause an unbearable dualism between two gods? For the moment we will postpone this question. For we have in this context been led to the existence of Satan only through the question as to whether the separation from God in which we live is fate or guilt. We shall therefore limit ourselves here to what the fact that we have to reckon with the reality of an opposing satanic power means for our relationship to God. Therefore we have to ask the question: if there is a satanic power, what relationship has then the satanic will to our will?

We saw that the diabolic power enters into the same level on which God is. To understand the way in which the satanic will is related to our own will we first have to see how God moves our will, what kind of relation comes into being between God's will and our will, when we act in God's charter. A man who, even if only once in his life, has acted or spoken in the certainty, "God wills it", knows that God's will is not in the same relationship to our will as other wills on the earthly level are. God does not force and enslave me from without, He does not press me like all wills to which I am in a polar relation of tension. If I act by divine legitimation, I act in the deepest freedom of will. *Servitium dei est summa libertas*: the service of God is perfect freedom. My will rests in God's command as in its *original* element. All cramped conditions and forced relations are dissolved as soon as the sacred "must" has come over me. That is so because God is the supra-polar Reality in which I am with my real being.

If incomprehensibly there is a satanic power which acts as God's antagonist and attempts to meet God on the same level of supra-polar existence, then this power presumes for itself what is proper to God alone. It breaks into the relationship that exists between God's will and my will when I act by God. It is therefore also true of the diabolical will that it is not a power that forces me from without but a will that takes possession of my inner being, a will that wills within me.

If this is the case then I cannot exculpate myself for my enmity to God by blaming Satan, and say: he has forced me. That would be possible if Satan were a factor of power within this world and influenced me as a power from without, as another man exercises pressure upon me. But the satanic power too is present in a supra-polar manner. It is not an extraneous will. It wills within my inner being. What I do by it is at the same time my own fault. I cannot exculpate myself by putting the blame on something or someone outside myself.

Herein we have realised the three truths which are given if we believe Christ when He says that there is a satanic power. If we recapitulate the three truths we have the answer to the question whether the separation from God in which we live is fate or guilt. Every one of us must say: I cannot attribute the fact that I am severed from God and therefore blind to Him, undecided in my decisions, suffering from life and afraid of death, to something which has been done to me, e.g. my human make-up, my physical and sensuous nature, my limited and temporal existence, my struggle for life. All that does not excuse me. For if I were in communion with God as I ought to be, then God could so reveal Himself to me that I could know Him. Then my body would be a temple of His Spirit, then the temporal form in which I live would no longer be a misery but a gift of grace. Then I would so rest in God's will, from which comes all that confronts me, that the suffering of life would be exalted in gratitude. My being far from God therefore can have no reason in anything that is outside my will. There is simply no explanation or excuse for it. That I am severed from God is my own fault, my own guilt, a deep and infinite guilt. It can be attributed to a satanic will which wills within me and rebels against God.

I realise this as soon as I am in God's presence. As long as this is not the case, I do not notice it and can in some way or other find a theological or philosophical interpretation of my lack of certainty. But as soon as I am in God's presence, I notice in myself an active enmity against God, for which there simply is no excuse. If this rebellion against God is to be found anywhere at all, then it cannot be limited to one place in the world. For it is directed against God. It has therefore a total character. A will to destroy God is rebellion on the whole front. Therefore, in the presence of God, when I pray to Him or receive a task from Him, it at once becomes clear to me that the anti-godly will that makes me unclean before God is found not only in me but in all that lives. Isaiah confesses in God's presence: "I am a man of unclean lips and I dwell in the midst of a people of unclean lips" (Is. VI.5). The Psalmist prays: "Enter not into judgment with thy servant, for no man living is righteous before thee" (Ps. CXLIII.2). Paul says that we are God's "enemies" as long as we have not been reconciled to Him by His wondrous intervention (Rom. V.10). Enmity always means mortal enmity. The enemy seeks to destroy his opponent. If we are God's enemies we participate in a rebellion to destroy God.

All these are no dogmatic statements, arrived at by speculation. On the contrary they break out with elementary power in prayer, in the man who feels God's presence. The fact that this is a collective movement against God does not take away my personal guilt but makes it even more serious. For this will that wills in all is not the will of an extraneous being that brings pressure to bear upon me. On the contrary it has supra-polar presence. While it wills in all it is at the same time altogether my own personal will for which I am fully responsible.

By stating all this we have merely developed what is contained in the statement of Jesus that there is a satanic power which rebels against God's sole dominion. As yet we have not endeavoured to enter with full understanding into the difficult truth expressed by this and into the questions which arise as

soon as we attempt to think out this truth to the end. Even if
at first we gather the words of Jesus about the Satan merely
as a fact from the sources of the New Testament, it is at once
obvious to us, what tremendous consequences it must have for
our entire view of the world, whether or not we follow the lead
of Jesus in this decisive point.

This is not merely a theological question. It brings to light
an ultimate contrast between two views of life, a contrast that
shows itself in all aspects of life and with which we are confronted again and again whenever we have to make decisions
in the political or economic sphere or in Church life. If we
deny the satanic, if therefore we do not take into account the
fact that within and around us there is a demoniacal opposition
against God, then it can be only due to misunderstanding when
people drag the sacred through the mire and fight against
purity and truth. The reason can only be that the ideal has
been so misrepresented to them that their healthy vital instincts
have revolted. Then Bolshevist anti-religious propaganda can
be explained by the fact that to the suppressed working man
belief in God must appear as a measure of the capitalist class
to comfort the exploited workers by an imaginary hereafter.
The anti-religious movement therefore is not aimed at God but
at the hypocritical abuse of His name which was already an
abomination to the Old Testament prophets. Then we must
be convinced that all men would at once gladly surrender to
God and glow with enthusiasm for purity and truth, as soon as
God is presented to them only in pure and shining colours
without distortion by the vulgar and fanatical people who on
earth pose as the representatives of His cause.

If therefore nations tear each other to pieces and individuals
exploit one another and persecute one another with hatred and
slander, this must be due to an unfortunate error. Men have
as yet not seen that by doing so they only harm themselves.
Consequently there is only one thing we need do to put an end
to the harm: we must enlighten the people. By comprehensive
mass education and suitable instruction we must clear away the
rubble of errors, due to false education, demagogic instigation
and priestly fanaticism. Then the pure flame of faith and love
will flare up automatically in all men. The nations will forge
their swords into ploughshares. Class-enmity and exploitation

will cease and men will fall into each other's arms as brethren.

Our judgment of life and our interpretation of history will become quite different if Jesus is right, if therefore we have to reckon with the reality of satanic power. Then the whole world outlook of the age of reason is the philosophy of an *anima candida* ("white soul") that still looks upon the world with a child's eyes and has as yet no idea of reality because it has not looked into its abysmal depths. Only when we reckon with the reality of satanic power have we woken up from the child's belief and are standing on reality. Only then does our prayer attain to the burning seriousness and urgency of Jesus' prayer at Gethsemane, and the prayers of Luther in his most difficult days. Here we see with alarming clarity the real reason why people reject God is not that the message concerning Him is distorted by dubious witnesses, fanatical prophets and mendacious priests and is compromised through intermixture with antiquated economic ordinances. On the contrary these things are no more than a very welcome pretext, which the opponents eagerly use to mask their attack on God by effective slogans and to clothe themselves in the cloak of culture and social justice. It is a serious error if we believe that people would turn to God in masses, if all offences were removed which have been caused by the human representatives of God's cause, and if only unselfish messengers like St. Francis went through the world in complete poverty and active love. On the contrary, the purer and the more unselfish the witnesses to the truth, the more the hatred of God flares up. When Jesus went through the country helping and healing, the demons everywhere broke forth against Him and uttered blasphemies. Him particularly, who did not seek anything for Himself, the world could not bear. The opposing satanic power did not rest until it had crucified Him. The first Christians, whose poor congregations were not yet tainted with any link with capitalism or with a tyrannical priesthood, were hated by the world of their time with the utmost violence and thrust out of society as *odium generis humani*. People did not just laugh with superior calm at this little circle of believers in God as childish dreamers; the authorities were not just content to see that their visionary illusions did not disturb public order. No, men hated these childlike people with a fanatical hatred and thought out increasingly cruel tortures to wear them down and to force them to defection. Christian virgins before their martyrdom in the arena were exposed to the lusts of the praetorians. How satanic that is!

Not until we take into account the reality of the diabolical power, are our eyes opened to the dark connexions between the age of the machine, capitalism, housing misery, factory labour by mothers, alcoholism, prostitution and destructive venereal diseases. We get a suspicion of the reason why it is the poisons which are most sure to ruin people, like opium, morphia and alcohol, that lure our senses with demonic sweetness and entice us to destruction with siren songs. The concrete experience of the world of God's champions like Luther leads them to the pessimistic impression which continually breaks forth in Luther's writings.

It may suffice here to refer to the material that is collected in Germannus Obendiek's book *Der Teufel bei Martin Luther*. "However one looks at it, he is the prince of the world. He who does not know this, try; I have some experience of it: but no one will believe me unless he experiences it for himself."[1] "The devil is lord in the world, and I myself could never really believe this, until I have now thoroughly experienced, that this too is an article of faith: *princeps mundi, deus huius seculi*."[2] "We are here in the realm of the devil, exactly as if a pilgrim came to an inn where he knew that they were all robbers: if he had to go there he would prepare himself and take measures as well as he could and not sleep very much. In the same way we are here on earth where the evil spirit is prince and has the hearts of men in his power and through them does what he pleases."[3] "I declare that the whole world is possessed of Satan."[4]

---

[1] Erlangen edn., VOL. XXX, p. 20.
[2] Weimar edn., VOL. L, p. 473.
[3] Weimar edn., VOL. XII, p. 384.
[4] Weimar edn., VOL. XLIII, p. 123.

CHAPTER 11

The Conflict between the Divine and the Satanic

IF UNDER the guidance of Jesus we reckon with the reality of the satanic we have to realise in advance, that therein a truth has been expressed which to our understanding is an insoluble contradiction. This contradiction is not a theological invention. Each of these two contradictory statements follows with equal necessity as soon as we endeavour to live in God's presence. This will first have to be shown in detail.

1. It belongs to the essence of God that He works all in all. Only if this is the case can God be our ultimate support, the Power from whose hand we can take everything. If there is anything at all in which God does not work, something that is outside His dominion, then God is no longer God. God has been dragged down into the polar relationships in which our human struggle for life is fought. God has become a factor of power within the world, who competes with other powers. Therefore if we stand before God in prayer, we cannot fathom and bear the thought that there is a Satan without, with Luther, making the other statement: God as the omnipresent is "present even in the devil".[1] The devil is merely "God's devil", i.e. an instrument of God. Luther makes God say to him: "Devil, you are a murderer and a scoundrel, but I shall use you for what I desire; you will be my scythe, the world and all that cleaves to you will be my manure for my beloved vineyard, that this may become all the better. . . . I will and I shall have you as my instrument for the vine, that it may be worked and prepared: therefore cut, raze and hoe, but no further than I want."[2] There is therefore no reason to shake the fundamental conviction on which our confidence in God rests, that God "does all things". All creatures are the disguises under which God hides. "He is present everywhere, in death, in hell, in the

---

[1] Obendiek, *Der Teufel bei Martin Luther*, Berlin 1931, p. 45.
[2] *Op. cit.*, p. 49.

midst of enemies, indeed even in their heart. For he has made all and also rules all. So that it must do what he pleases." Luther does not shrink from the final consequence which follows: God is also present in the devil, and not merely as a spectator, but actively. For as soon as anywhere God is not active but merely a spectator, He is dethroned: "*Quando deus omnia movet et agit, necessario movet etiam et agit in Satana et in impio* (As God moves and acts in all things, He necessarily also moves and acts in Satan and in the impious man)."

If we cannot say this in faith, then our faith in God is shaken in its foundations. For if God has a rival who puts His dominion over the world in question, then there is no God at all. Then the world is a battlefield on which two relative and limited powers measure their strength, or two generals lead their armies against each other. God Himself is then in the arena in which the struggle of nations and men is fought with changing success. He is no longer the Ruler of battles who is above the parties. He is no longer the Lord of the world but like Alexander or Napoleon a conqueror of the world for whom there are still unconquered countries and unvanquished enemies. If this is the case then God is not the One to whom we can have recourse in all needs, as Luther says in his explanation of the first commandment.[3]

Therefore nothing must be deducted from the truth that God "does all things", that we have to praise and thank Him for all that happens. Otherwise belief in God loses all its strength. Otherwise we are not, in all that happens to us, dealing with God. When after Absalom's rising the old family hatred and thirst for revenge against David broke forth in Shimei of Saul's family, and he threw stones at the fugitive king and swore at him: "Begone, begone, you man of blood!" David said, "Let him alone, and let him curse; for the Lord has bidden him" (II Sam. XVI.11). David did not say: God has allowed the enemy to give vent to his anger with me, as during a riot the police for some time look on with crossed arms while two groups of men assault each other with clubs and interfere only when they start to break windows. If God looks on in this way while men vent their rage against me, and only reserves the right to interfere in case of emergency and to take police-measures,

[3] Weimar edn., VOL. VI, pp. 204-14; Clemen, VOL. I, pp. 229-41.

then I am not under the stone-throws of my enemies dealing with God but am abandoned to the fury of men. God may be a Power stronger than all men; but in this case He is just the same merely a relative and limited power. I am not dealing with Him alone. God is only my God, if all that happens to me really does come from Him. Only if the latter is the case, then, under the lowest maledictions and slander of the enemy venting his malignity and rancour on me, can I say with David: "Let him alone, and let him curse; for the Lord has bidden him." Job receives the message that those low predatory vagabonds, the Sabeans, have made an attack on his peacefully grazing herds, stolen his cows and asses and put the servants to the sword: "Then Job arose, and rent his mantle and said: 'The Lord gave, and the Lord has taken away; blessed be the name of the Lord'" (Job 1.21). He does not say: The Lord has allowed it to happen, He has not prevented the gang of robbers from giving full vent to their greed and bloodthirstiness, God has watched how it happened from heaven, though He could have interfered with lightning and thunder. In this case Job would not really have been dealing with God but just with human depravity permitted by God. He can bear the terrible blow only if he can genuinely say: the Lord has taken away, God was the One who took away. The robbers and murderers in their cowardly attack were the instruments through whom God took away from Job what He wished to take away. In the same sense Jesus, in the hour when Satan had taken possession of Judas and the armed crowd surrounded Him on all sides, says: "Shall I not drink the cup which the Father has given me?" (Jn. XVIII.11). The Father therefore has not merely allowed the dark power to give vent to its fury against Him, the Father has given Him the cup. The Father was giving and active from the beginning until the end.

The man who has to learn to keep faith in the most difficult situation, physically broken, slandered and dishonoured by men, abandoned to an excruciating death, knows that everything depends on whether it is wholly true, without qualification, that all things come from God and that God works even in the satanic so that even when fighting with the power of the devil we are dealing only with God. In such a situation the really serious temptation, as Luther knew only too well, is the thought: God has withdrawn from me; I no longer experience his presence and am abandoned without defence to the power of darkness. As soon as this impression arises, we lose our last support and break down. It is all-important that we should hold on to this: God who works all in all, also works in Satan.

2. For the same reason, because otherwise we lose God, we have to say equally clearly the second thing, which to our human thinking contradicts the first. As soon as we make only the one statement, that the devil is a subordinate creature, a minor functionary in God's court like Goethe's Mephistopheles, merely a harmless instrument of the one God who works all in all, then we have misjudged the seriousness of our situation and distorted according to our own wishes the picture of the reality in which we are placed. The temptation of Jesus and His agony at Gethsemane would have been a mere fight against windmills, a sham fight against an impotent opponent, whom a man with God behind him could not take seriously at all, if it were not true that at that moment God's cause really was at stake; He who represented God's cause was meeting with a mortal enemy, whom He took completely seriously. Therefore we also have to state the terrible thesis, whether we can understand it or not: there is a dark power which wishes to dethrone God and it is not a matter of course that this power is vanquished. All God's witnesses, who gave their lives for Him, have known this sinister fact. They noticed the invisible enemy within themselves and in the decisive steps of their lives they felt persecuted by him.

Paul knew that he was beaten by a messenger of Satan (II Cor. XII.7). In other words he experienced the physical vexations which hindered him in the execution of his apostolic office as lashes of the devil. He wanted to forgive a man at Corinth who had badly offended him "to keep Satan from gaining the advantage over us; for we are not ignorant of his designs" (II Cor. II.11). He delivered the fornicator unto Satan (I Cor. V.5). He had a strong desire again to see his church at Thessalonica and twice tried to visit her, "but Satan hindered us" (I Thess. II.18). Luther too had the same conviction that the Satan continually endeavoured to hinder him in the execution of his divine task.

CHAPTER 12

The Two Incompatible Comprehensive Views by which the Belief in God lives

ALL THE WITNESSES to God have known this: God cannot be made responsible for that which comes between God and us, for the will of enmity against God within us all. It cannot be attributed to anything that comes from God, neither to our human constitution, nor to the form of existence of the world, nor to the dialectic relationship between time and eternity. It is entirely our own inexcusable fault. But because this will rebels against God it cannot be a mere limited human will. It is rather the will of a power which wants to enter into the same level as God.

We must make it clear to ourselves why the two statements made above follow of necessity, as soon as we are not reflecting theologically on the essence of God but have to act responsibly under the guidance of Jesus in the presence of God.

1. Firstly the statement, that our being far from God is our own fault for which we ourselves are solely responsible before God. Again and again in the history of spiritual development the attempt has been made to exclude the satanic and to put the blame for the anti-godly movement of the creature on God Himself. This was already done in the old-reformed supralapsarian doctrine of predestination, according to which God had brought about the fall of the creature in order to glorify Himself. But the thought arises even more ingeniously and bewitchingly in German speculative philosophy. God posits His own antithesis to take it back in a higher form. Or as Schleiermacher puts it: the evil has been ordained in corporate human life as a gateway to the good![1] This romantic glorification of the demonic appears continually as a mood in contemporary poetry, e.g. in the well-known poem *Drei Ringe* by

[1] *Glaubenslehre*, par. 83; *Christian Faith*, pp. 341-5.

Richard Dehmel. The three rings remind the poet of three broken promises:

> *Ach! Immer die Treue treuwillig versprochen,*
> *und immer treuwillig die Treue gebrochen.*
> *So hat es das Leben, das Leben gewollt. . . .*
> *Die Freiheit verschworen, die Freiheit verloren.*
> *So hat es die Liebe, die Liebe gewollt. . . .*
> *Raum! Raum! brich Bahnen, wilde Brust!*
> *Ich fühl's und staune jede Nacht,*
> *dass nicht bloss eine Sonne lacht;*
> *das Leben is des Lebens Lust!*
> *Hinein, hinein mit blinden Händen,*
> *du hast noch nie das Ziel gewusst;*
> *zehntausend Sterne, aller Enden,*
> *zehntausend Sonnen stehn und spenden*
> *uns ihre Strahlen in die Brust!*

("Ah! Ever faithfully pledged the troth / and ever faithfully broken the pledge. / That is how life, life has willed it! . . . / Freedom promised, freedom lost. / That is how love, love, has willed it! . . . / Room! Room! Make way, wild breast! / I feel it and am amazed every night / that there is not merely *one* Sun smiling; / Life is the joy of Life! / Enter, enter with blind seeking hands / never yet have you known the end; / ten thousand stars everywhere, / ten thousand suns are there and send their rays into our breast!")

Here "life", "love", the world's riches of sunshine are made responsible for the broken promises. In this way the blame is put on the Creator who has placed us in a world full of suns. God acquires "diabolical characteristics" (Schlatter). We realise at once what this means in practice when we are confronted with a dangerous moral temptation in which the lusts drag us down as winding plants drag down a swimmer, so that only by exerting all our will-power can we stay afloat. We realise the danger that arises if in this situation the thought comes up: to exhaust the full riches of God's created world I also have to sink into the night and the abysses of life; for God Himself has ordained this opposing pole to His essence as a necessary thoroughfare to the fulfilment of His creation. *Eritis sicut deus.* "You will be like God, knowing good and evil" (Gen. III.5). As soon as we are intoxicated with this thought,

our will to resistance is broken. This thought works like frater-
nisation in the trenches in the middle of a battle. For why
should we make sacrifices, deny ourselves pleasures and risk our
lives to destroy an enemy who after all has a divine right to
exist because he is necessary for the full unfolding of God's
riches? We feel clearly that this enticing thought puts the
entire seriousness of morality in question. The sacredness of
every duty and responsibility is at stake. For the ultimate
exertion of our will in the fight against evil is only possible if
there is something that absolutely has to be fought and vanquished, something for which there is simply no excuse. This
is the case only if God and Satan are absolute and irreconcilable
enemies, between whom there is no connexion, no cease-fire,
no mediation.

Karl Holl, in the first essay of the book in which he has
endeavoured to expose the deepest levels of Luther's faith,
makes one false step and wonders if Luther should not ultimately have embraced the divine and the satanic in one higher
comprehensive idea. Holl says it would have been obvious in
connexion with evil to conclude that God must bring forth
evil, thereby to awaken the consciousness of good, the conscience
of mankind.[2] Schleiermacher really drew this conclusion in
his *Glaubenslehre*: The evil has been ordained in corporate
human life as a gateway to the good.[3] But Holl is too con-
scientious an historian not to add at once: Luther did not go
so far as to draw this conclusion. He was evidently afraid that
by such an admission all moral concepts would lose their
strictness. However it was not merely fear, as Holl says, that
kept Luther from applying the easy formula: the good is *opus
proprium dei* (God's proper work), the evil is *opus alienum* (foreign)
dei. Luther had this easy formula at hand, but he did not
apply it, not merely because of a certain reserve; no, something
greater was at stake here. Everything was at stake here. The
important thing was that here no effort should be made
to harmonise. Otherwise all that Luther had gained would
have been lost. This is the high tension of Luther's entire
theology. Any effort to detract from the antinomy one way or

---

[2] Karl Holl, *Gesammelte Aufsätze zur Kirchengeschichte*, VOL. I, Tübingen 1921,
pp. 1-90: "Was verstand Luther unter Religion?"

[3] *Glaubenslehre*, par. 83; *Christian Faith*, pp. 341-5.

the other would have robbed everything of the value of being true to life.

2. If in the presence of God we ponder on His essence then the second statement inevitably follows; that the will of enmity against God that lives in us is not a limited human will but a supra-human omnipresent will which desires to enter into the place where God is. Why is it that rebellion against God, even if it starts from a weak human will, at once assumes super-human proportions and a demoniacal character and aims at the destruction of God?

This thought would not arise if the Being against whom we revolt were a relative and limited being. If we were dealing with a relative being, e.g. another man, then it is no attack on the existence of this other creature if its influence on me is limited, if in the important things of my life I retain my independence of it. I can be excluded from a human "thou" without his existence being put in question. But it is a different case when I have a broken relationship with God. For God is God only if at every moment all that is is determined by Him and rests in Him. "From him and through him and to him are all things" (Rom. xi.36). If in the whole realm of all that exists there is something, only at one spot, that withdraws from Him, then this is not merely a minor disturbance which has no further meaning and has no influence at all on the relationship between God and the world, as a minor riot in a provincial town which is at once broken up by the police cannot shake the central government. The case is much more serious because this is not a human government but God. As Anselm formulated it correctly, divinity means that all that exists beside God exists for God. If therefore in the realm of all that is something arises that is not there for God but exists beside Him, then there is a cabinet crisis. God's divinity, God's being God is at stake. For if anything at all is exempt from the sole dominion of God then God has been degraded to a relative power on the same level as the other factors of power in this world, which mutually qualify and limit each other. God's power may still be stronger than the other forces which compete with Him. But nevertheless, as soon as even at one spot its sphere of influence is limited, then it has been degraded to a relative worldly power and there is no divinity left.

That we reserve the name of "God" for Him by whom at every moment all things are is not just a theological construction. On the contrary: this is the only basis on which we can call upon God in every situation. For we can only pray, if we accept the whole destiny of our lives from His hands and are able to say: "Nothing can happen to me but what God has chosen and is beneficial to me." If the sole agency of God has any limits at all, in other words if it is limited by factors within the world, then my destiny is no longer under God's guidance. Then a large number of factors have collaborated to shape this destiny, an incalculable number of natural influences and human plans, and God has merely occasionally interfered with their operation and execution. If in the total realm of all that is something happens that does not entirely come from God, then God is no longer "That to which one should look confidently for all good and to which one should have recourse in all needs."[4]

What follows for our situation? If anywhere in the vast realm of creation some being withdraws from God and lives far from Him, then this is not a harmless event but – in God's presence we realise this at once – an attack on His reality. As Anselm declares: If anywhere in the universe anyone casts only one glance in a direction contrary to God's will, then the divinity of God is in every respect put in question. God is opposed by a power which not merely wishes to limit, but to dethrone Him. Therefore as soon as we come under the power of an unclean desire, it envelops us in a night in which we do not even see God any longer. The nearer God has been to us before, the more keenly we experience this. He who has never yet in his life met God as an inescapable Reality will of course reject all that has been said about the satanic background of even the slightest rebellion against Him as fantastic mythology.

Summing up all that has been said, we have made it clear that as soon as we not merely think about the essence of God but live by faith in Him, two comprehensive views always arise, which we simply cannot harmonise. The first view we call the standpoint of God's sole agency. According to it God works all in all, the devil is merely "God's devil". The other view we call the standpoint of conflict. According to this God is at

[4] Weimar edn., VOL. XXX, 1, pp. 133-4; Clemen, VOL. IV, pp. 4-5.

war with an opposing power which encounters Him as a mortal enemy on the level of supra-polar existence. And genuine, deep faith, proved by the fire of temptation, shows itself in the co-existence of the two views, equally unqualified, in the fact that no attempt is made to harmonise them, indeed that any interpenetrating comprehensive view is instinctively rejected as a dangerous temptation.

Otherwise, if one can prove to a man that his statements contradict one another, he does all that he can to eliminate the contradiction. For a man has been refuted as soon as he can be convinced that he has contradicted himself. It is the most mortal weapon in intellectual combat, if I can prove to my opponent that he has got mixed up in contradiction and that today he says the opposite of what he said yesterday. The victim will try anything to get out of the scrape and to solve the contradiction supposed to be found in his views. Here we meet with the opposite attitude. Genuine faith in God bears with the contradiction that arises when it attempts to express its content in human words and thoughts. The contradiction does not break it. It knows that it cannot solve the contradiction by itself. God alone can solve it, and He will do so when faith is changed into vision. The contradiction can be borne with only in this eschatological certitude. Therefore every attempt to eliminate the contradiction in a human way must be checked. Faith in God has its world-conquering power only so long as it retains the high tension of this contradiction, of which the solution is awaited from God with burning expectation. Its dynamic power is lost as soon as any attempt is made to isolate one of the two comprehensive views and to set it over the other, or dialectically to co-ordinate the two contradictory standpoints in one interpenetrating inclusive comprehensive view.

If we isolate the comprehensive view of God's sole agency, if we speak only of the Father who clothes the lilies and cares for the birds and arranges all things for the good of his children, if we make the devil a harmless goblin who does subordinate work in the house of God the Father, then the man who "in this mercilessly icy world" fights the battle that decides about life and death senses that this cheerful optimism is contrary to the reality in which he himself lives. He cannot do anything with this philosophy. He feels it as a mockery of his own situation. It seems to him like the philosophy of Sunday-children who have been born on the sunny side of life. He can only accept a philosophy in which the demoniacal powers have a place as realities which have to be taken seriously. But conversely if we isolate the comprehensive view of the conflict between divine and satanic power, without this being balanced by the view of God's sole agency, then we lose the support that we particularly need in the hottest struggle for life, the outside point by which the whole world of polarities can be lifted off its hinges. Consequently it is all-important that the two standpoints are retained side by side, like two heavy weights keeping each other in balance.

That there is a contradiction on which we do not break but by which we live, that the two contradictory theses do not mutually destroy each other like two trains colliding at full speed, is possible only in a state of mind which we cannot reach by our own strength, the possibility of which we can no longer follow with our thought. If we want to describe this state of mind we must clearly distinguish between the thought-expressions to which we are led if we conceptually describe it, and the thing under discussion itself, that is to say the relation into which thereby we enter with our whole existence.

When describing "spaces" in Vol. I[5] we saw that to *be* in a relation, e.g. in three-dimensional cubic space, is something different from the attempt we must make to *formulate* the relation between the third dimension and the two-dimensional plane and the one-dimensional extent. We can be in cubic space without thinking about it and without being able to describe by words and concepts the miracle that we experience when, born blind, we become able to see. It is the same with being in the ultimate relation which is both at the same time: to rest in God who works all in all, and to join in the struggle between God and Satan. Standing in this double relation is an existence, the reality of which is a fact, independent of whether or not we are capable of conceptually describing it.

Men who reckoned with the reality of God therefore have always had the need of finding a special word for this incomprehensible relationship, a word that is used only here as the

[5] *God Transcendent* (pp. 60-1, 90).

radical word that contains all that we can say about the ultimate things. This is the word *faith* as contrasted to *vision* which
embraces all that can be experienced and imagined within the
framework of the polar relationships of this world. The *sola
fides* of the German Reformation, according to its original
meaning, means neither *accepting as true*, nor *trusting*, in fact no
activity of the soul at all, which could be made the object of
psychological research, but something far more fundamental
that is prior to any functions of cognition or volition. It means
that with our whole existence we are in a relationship which is
at a deeper level than all our psychological functions, in which
our certainty as regards the ultimate conditions of thinking and
willing is anchored, from which therefore our deepest knowledge
and the deepest decisions of our will grow, as a tree with wide-
spread branches grows from a hidden root which lives under
the surface.

If with our thinking we wish to understand and contemplate
the *original* relation in which we have been placed by faith,
then it is as if we try to look with our eyes into the *original* light
of the sun. It blinds us. If our reflexion wishes conceptually
to understand the *original* relation, it breaks on the latter. It
breaks into two incompatible comprehensive views: the mon-
istic view of God's sole activity and the dualistic view of a
contest between two powers wrestling with each other. To
stand in the *original* relation is the incomprehensible certainty
that the two views, incongruous to our thinking, together
nevertheless form an inseparable unity, although our "Euclidean mind" cannot grasp how this is possible. It is clear that
we can neither reach this certainty by our experience nor
invent it by our intellect. God Himself alone can grant it. As
one who believes in God I know that God holds me over the
abyss of enmity against God within me and around me. From
hour to hour God carries me as on eagle's wings above the unfathomable depths of the demoniacal world and of my own
God-resisting heart. Even though I cannot understand how
this is possible, I know that nothing can separate me from the
love of God, no one can snatch me out of His hand, although
the strongest powers in the world have bound themselves with
oaths that they will separate me from Him.

CHAPTER 13

Original Sin and Individual Sin[1]

WE MUST have realised that the *original* relation which is the unity of this infinite tension passes understanding, that our cognition is blinded if it attempts to look into this mystery. For only then can we find our position as regards the particular questions which arise as soon as we speak of an *original* sin, which weighs on all of us and to which the condition in which we live of being far from God must be attributed. One asks first of all – this question has been the subject of lively discussion, especially since the publication of Karl Holl's book on Luther – how I can be held responsible for something that after all is not due to a conscious decision of my will which I have made knowing very well that I could equally have decided for the opposite. It is not a result of conscious apostasy that God is not an undoubted Reality to me and that I do not live by Him in such a way that I need not continually seek the way back to Him in prayer; I cannot remember ever having been in any other situation. We all have the impression that when our consciousness awoke we were already living in this condition of being far from God. Can I be convicted of something for which I have not made a conscious decision? Can an inner attitude which I have not consciously chosen be anything else but fate, destiny, a disease? Can this be called guilt?

To give an answer to this question we have to remember that, as we have seen before, the ethical categories of guilt and responsibility belong to the sphere of the *original* relation. For we can become guilty only in relation to a power which can make an absolute demand on us. If the *original* relation is beyond our cognition then the same applies to guilt and responsibility. The consciousness of guilt is an *original* experience beyond which we cannot reach with our reflexion. We cannot dispose of our conscience. It does not depend on us whether

---

[1] The usual expression *actual sin* obscures the issue. Tr.

something weighs on our conscience as guilt or not. If something troubles our conscience, then no reflexion can remove the consciousness of guilt weighing on it. Neither we nor anyone else, as a priest or a psychiatrist, can rid us of the burden by a decision of will or an argument of reason. Conversely if we have a clear conscience over some action, then we cannot work ourselves up to a consciousness of guilt by autosuggestion, nor can the most bitter reproaches by other people or the severest punishment by the highest human tribunal arouse any consciousness of guilt in us.

This means that neither the arousing nor the removal of the consciousness of guilt is in our power. Therefore it is also impossible reflectively to decide once and for all, on the basis of our experience so far, which conditions must be fulfilled and what the situation must be for any consciousness of guilt to arise. The latter would mean an anticipation of the course of events and an attempt to draw up a permanent rule according to which alone a consciousness of guilt could arise. We have no right to do that. There are only two things we can do. Firstly we can wait for what happens to us in this field, in which we have no say. And secondly, when we have had experiences of guilt we can condense those experiences into principles.

If we maintain that we can be held responsible only for something on which we have consciously decided, then this assertion can only have the value of a principle derived from experience, in which we condense the experiences which we have had within a limited field of observation. We are then thinking of cases in our lives, in which we were burdened with a particularly heavy load of conscience because with open eyes we rushed into destruction, knowing full well that the mistake could equally well have been avoided. Such cases have certainly occurred and the memory of them is particularly fresh. But this does not mean that we are justified in concluding that consciousness of guilt can arise only in such cases. If there is only one case to which this concept of guilt based on those blatant cases does not apply, then it is proved that our concept of guilt is too narrow.

Luther and Melanchthon pointed to a fact that people have since again and again confirmed by their experience. What burdens our conscience when we are standing before God, is not in the first place the decisions in life which we have taken deliberately after calm and serious consideration of all the contrasting possibilities. In such cases all those ethical prohibitions and "drills" (*Dressate*)[2] which we owe to our ethical education usually come into force. These bridle our strong natural instincts and protect us against mistakes. We are much more upset in our conscience by inclinations in connexion with which these prohibitions do not work. These are inclinations which occur entirely involuntarily, before any ethical consideration can set in.

Some examples from life: I receive a message that a business competitor who has been my rival for years has met with a motor accident and has been taken to hospital with serious injuries. My first reaction is malicious joy. Immediately after this ethical considerations set in, and prohibitions due to education become active. I am ashamed of my mean feeling. I am really sorry for the man and with sincere sympathy inquire from his relations how he is. A second example. A gifted young man who has always put me in the shade by his successes, has received a position which makes him famous at once. The first thing I experience on receiving this news is envy. Immediately afterwards my good moral education comes into force. I am sorry I have allowed myself such a mean feeling. My better ego becomes prevalent. I no longer begrudge my young friend his success and hurry to congratulate him with all my heart. In both cases we are dealing with inclinations which are prior to any conscious decision. They arise in me entirely involuntarily, before my conscious will comes into effect.

The question now arises: can we, because there is no question here of any conscious decision of the will, decline all responsibility for these nasty inclinations of malicious joy, envy, hatred and rage? Are we innocent of them? Are we in the same relation to them as we are to an illness or a physical pain, which attacks us without our provocation so that we cannot blame ourselves for it? We manifestly do not manage to regard them in this way. On the contrary, it is particularly these entirely instinctive and involuntary inclinations of mean professional, commercial and artistic rivalry, of outright, almost sadistic malicious joy in the misery of someone else, which arise

[2] F. Künkel.

in me during the first unguarded moments, that make me feel even more ashamed than wrong decisions taken after clear deliberation. I am shocked at the abysmal meanness which reveals itself in these feelings, and of which I had not thought myself capable. But I cannot accept the dark instincts to which I am subject indifferently as if they were merely a fate. I know only too well that they are the impulses of my own heart. I feel stained by them. I regret them as one regrets a fault.

To everyone who, because of his own experience, admits this fact, this is a refutation of the assertion that we can feel guilty only of something on which we have decided with full consciousness. It has been shown that in every-day life, it is true, the responsibility for conscious decisions takes first place and now as before retains its great importance. But consciousness of guilt is something far more comprehensive and far less transparent than we thought at first. Underneath the feeling of guilt that comes into being more or less before our eyes, in the daylight of our consciousness, there is a guilt which belongs to the dark depths of our being and rises to the surface of our daylight-consciousness only at extraordinary moments. This guilt is to be found in the instinctive proclivities and impulses which run within us like subterranean rivers. Even if it is only in a few cases in every-day life that we feel guilty of instinctive impulses which have not arisen from conscious decisions, nevertheless it is proved that we have understood the concept of guilt far too superficially and rationalistically if we try to limit it to those cases where, like Hercules at the crossroads, we have the choice between various possibilities. On the contrary there is a guilt to which we are subject before any conscious deliberation has set in.

If we have to admit this as a result of our own experience, then we can no longer safeguard ourselves by any theoretical objection, when in God's presence we realise the secret hatred of Him, the Promethean rebellion against the superior power of the Creator, in which we have been engaged since we have lived and have been able to think, and when this hidden enmity of our heart burdens our soul not as fate but as guilt. Indeed we have to go one step further and say that the awakening of the deeper consciousness of guilt, of our "hidden faults" (Ps. XIX.12), shows our conscious wrong decisions in a new

light as well. That I am capable at all of being disobedient to
a clearly known will of God is in itself something entirely
incomprehensible. It is possible only because a hidden enmity
towards God is living within me, from which the conscious
decisions grow as from a root. "The bad tree bears evil fruit"
(Mt. vii.17). Conscious decisions are merely the releasing
causes which actualise the hostile attitude that is hidden and
alive within me. Conscious sins therefore are merely secondary
reflexions of the primary *original* sin which we have before God;
and we have only a very shallow knowledge of ourselves if we
are prepared to accept responsibility for the fruits of the "bad
tree" but decline it for the existence of the tree on which the
fruit grows all the time.

This brings us to the second objection that is raised when
we regard the reality of a satanic power as the deepest ground
of our being far from God. One asks: is it not an essential
aspect of guilt and responsibility that the bearer of the guilt,
the subject responsible, is an individual person? How can I
conceivably ascribe the guilt to a satanic power which resists
God in every respect, and at the same time accept the guilt for
myself as an individual? This objection too we can raise only
as long as it has not dawned on us that guilt and responsibility
are relationships the origin of which we can never fathom
because they belong to the supra-polar sphere.

We saw in the first volume that even in the empirical world
which is immediately accessible to us, the non-objective ego,
the knowing and willing personality, remains unfathomable
and resistant to being made an object. Therefore we cannot by
our objective knowledge decide what relations are possible
between "I" and "thou". The border-line between "I" and
"thou", the dimensional unity and distinction between them,
can be expressed by our objective thought only as a paradox.[3]
That already brings us beyond the naïve conception that individuals stand beside each other like celestial bodies in the dark
universe, or are separated from each other as rooms in a
building are separated by walls, that is that they can only be
beside each other, never within each other.

These obscure relations between "I" and "thou" are placed
in an entirely new light as soon as we see the *original* relation

[3] *Glaube und Denken*, p. 160 (159).

of the polar world to the supra-polar existence of God. We discover ourselves only when God meets us, as it is said at the critical point of the story in the parable of the prodigal son: "He came to himself" (εἰς ἑαυτὸν δὲ ἐλθών, Lk. xv.17). In the presence of God we reach knowledge of ourselves and abandon the attempt to escape from ourselves. Only when we stand before God as the bearers of our guilt, responsible to Him, does it dawn on us in His presence, in what relationship we are to each other and what responsibility we have for one another.

In God's presence it also becomes clear to us, as we have already seen, that the will in us that rebels against God, itself wants to be god and occupy God's place. "If there were gods, who could then bear not to be god?"[4] This will which desires to dethrone God so as to put itself in His place desires to possess us as God does. He desires that we should be in him in the same way as we ought to be in God. If I am in God and speak and act on His command, in His power, then in an incomprehensible way two things happen: God has the responsibility for that which I do and for all the consequences which follow from it; and I myself under His command have become a responsible ego that stands before God and rests in His will in perfect freedom.

There are therefore two responsible authorities and yet these two responsible authorities are not only separate but at the same time also within one another. This is a relationship which would be entirely inconceivable within the polar relations of the world. But it is possible in the *original* relation.

The same holds good of the relationship between myself and the satanic power that drags me into rebellion against God. We speak of satanic possession. Thereby we mean the paradoxical fact that here too we have to say two things: (1) There are two responsible authorities. (2) But both authorities are within each other in the *original* relation. I therefore always have to admit, first that I alone am the guilty person, the prodigal son who without any apparent reason leaves the Father's house and goes abroad. But secondly I must say that the guilt belongs to the satanic will of rebellion, which wills not only in me but in millions of other beings and makes the mad attempt to throw God off His throne. When I look across the surface of a lotus

---

[4] Friedrich Nietzsche, *Also sprach Zarathustra*, PT. II, Chemnitz 1883, p. 6.

pond, I see separate leaves floating on the dark water, seemingly independent of each other. If I could look into the depth I would see that all these leaves are organically connected by long thin stems with a common root which grows from the soil in the dark depth at the bottom of the pond.

We have so far been developing what is entailed in the fact that Jesus reckons with a satanic power, that He knows that He is called "to destroy the works of the devil". The existence of this power, which has declared war on God, is the ultimate cause of the condition of being far from God in which we find ourselves. That is the reason why we have to seek God by prayer and meditation and to unite with other people into a congregation meeting at particular times in places of worship to be still and to seek an encounter with God. It simply would not occur to us to do such things if we were with God as we should be, if God were the "air that fills all, in which we ever move".

In the last chapters of the Revelation of John, in the Seer's description of the final state of things, the temple and all that goes with it has therefore disappeared, because the normal relation between God and the creature has been restored. "And I saw no temple in the city, for its temple is the Lord God the Almighty" (Rev. xxi.22). Temples, churches, chapels, forms of worship, holy days, common to all human religions, Aryan as well as Semitic, are therefore an expression of our being far from God, a sign that there is a power that drags us away from God down into godforsakenness, so that we have continually to lift ourselves up and make special efforts not to fall away from fellowship with God. We are like an aeroplane, which is continuously pulled down by its own weight, and needs a continuously working engine to keep itself in motion and in the air.

The law of gravity that drags us away from God down into the depth does not originate in some condition for which we are not responsible. The only ground for it is the rebellious will, hostile to God, that is alive in the deepest ground of our own being and for which there is no excuse. The nearer God comes to us and the more we come under His sway, the more noticeable this rebellion against God becomes. We experience it particularly forcibly when God wants to impose a hard destiny upon us, when God wills that we shall diminish and

die so that others may increase and live at our expense. We do
not want to submit to this. We resist God's will with all our
strength. The rebellious will also stirs when God gives us a
difficult task that takes away our power to determine our whole
life. In his astonishing confession the prophet Jeremiah relates
how he immediately rebelled on receiving the divine com-
mission and wished that God would not exist at all. "I say,
'I will not mention him, or speak any more in his name'"
(Jer. xx.9).

We cannot argue on theoretical grounds whether Jesus is
right, whether this unfounded and inexcusable satanic will of
rebellion against God exists, or whether it is merely the product
of a morbid imagination, explainable in terms of physical de-
generation. For the reality of the satanic is experienced only
in the consciousness of guilt which comes over us in the presence
of God. This experience of guilt, as we have seen, has its roots
in the infathomable depths of our being. We cannot dispose of
it. By reasoning we can neither bring it about nor do away
with it.

There are therefore only two possibilities. Either we declare
that, thanks be to God, in our experience of life so far we have
not noticed anything of this will that is hostile to God. Then
we can be glad and grateful, and we need not allow the harmony of our view of the world to be disturbed any further by
that dark phantom that darkened the lives of men like Jesus,
Paul and Luther. Or we have experienced that consciousness
of guilt. In spite of all our philosophical objections we have to
admit of this uncanny fact, because we are in our conscience
convinced of it. Then we must also draw all the consequences.
Then the reality of the satanic must not merely – as usually
happens in theological books – appear somewhere at the edge
of our view of the world, as a slight shadow which can only
emphasise the sunlight that shines on the whole but has no
serious import for the understanding of our vital situation. If
the diabolical power is a reality, then there is no aspect of life
for the understanding of which this fact is not of decisive
importance.

Accordingly we get a very one-sided and superficial picture
of all political and economic relationship, if we do not take
this decisive factor into account. But if we do reckon with it,

then wherever we go and are, where we work and suffer and affect other people, we are dealing not only with God but at the same time also with this dark opposing power. If this gigantic shadow of the satanic is cast over the entire world, then, if as theologians we want to develop a system of faith, we cannot start from the sin of the individual or from the fatal fall of mankind, which has its terrible effects in Promethean pride and Titanic presumption, in indelible self-sufficiency and self-assertion, in wars between nations and the economic exploitation of the weak. Then there is only one reason for the fact that the world is in need of deliverance. That reason is the inexplicable existence of a power which desires the destruction of God. Then all the things which make us unhappy, unharmonious, hard, cruel, ruthless and ungodly can only be the branches which grow from this one bitter root, the parts of a monstrous coherent battle-front, the movements of which are systematically directed from one hidden headquarters. If there is a salvation of the world then this salvation can ultimately not be concerned with the individual but with the question whether there can be a victory over the power of darkness, in which the enemy will really be defeated so that all the effects of the state of war will cease.

I

CHAPTER 14

Original Sin and the Form of the World

To MAKE CLEAR the central import of the fundamental fact which, according to the foregoing, forms the key to a biblical understanding of the world, we yet have to discuss a question which determines our attitude to the world. What is the relation between the *original* sin in which we all share and the form of the world in which we live? More precisely, what is the relation between the inexcusable state of being far from God, in which we are, and the polar form of existence of the empirical world of which we are part? Can we unconditionally and without reserve say "yes" to the world in which we are placed? Can we have a grateful positive approach to the reality with which we are dealing every day, the soil in which we sow the seed that it may give us bread, the metal that we dig from the mountain in order to melt it into the engines by which we dominate the earth, the child in the cradle that we nurse and tend because it bears the future of our race? Do we say an unqualified "yes" to the realities of the world? Or do we have a broken attitude to them, a "yes" contradicted by a "no", a "yes" that has passed through a "no"? Again and again we are told today that only an unbroken "yes" to this earth can bring forth complete devotion to the tasks which our terrestrial existence puts before us. At times when these tasks demand the sacrifice of our life, it is all-important that we can speak this "yes" without any mental reservation. Otherwise we also make a tacit reservation in relation to our willingness to sacrifice, and this reservation paralyses our devotion.

The answer to the question with which we are here confronted depends essentially on whether the *original* sin in which we share also casts a shadow on the form of the world or whether there is no direct connexion between *original* sin and the ordinances of this world. Two points of view contrast with one another. Some say that the world has come from the hand of the Creator pure and good. Therefore when at our birth we enter this world we are on sacred territory. Sacred are the natural laws of the organic world, sacred is the intercourse of the sexes if they fulfil the commandment of fertility. Sacred is the struggle for power by which clans, tribes and nations try their strength with one another so that the weak, cowardly and degenerate are destroyed and the strong and healthy carry the day. Sacred is death by which, when our time is up, we return our life to the Creator who gave it. Sacred is the *original* law of time according to which all things rise and fall, flower and decay in eternal change. Certainly human errors and sins do occur. But these minor deviations cannot disturb the great cycles of God's ordering of creation any more than children playing on the bank of a river and throwing pebbles which disturb the water, can stop or divert the current.

The opposite point of view is most simply expressed by the words of the Epistle to the Romans, taking them as they stand, for the time being without any explanation: "The wages of sin is death" (Rom. VI.23). "Sin came into the world through one man and death through sin, and so death spread to all men because all men sinned" (Rom. V.12). Here Paul points to the fundamental order which lends its character to the form of the world in which we live, viz. the universal fate of death of the organic world; he then connects this order and the guilt in which we all share. Similarly in the ninetieth Psalm the whole order of flowering and withering, the stream-like flowing that lends its form to our temporal existence, is connected with a guilt which we have on our conscience before God. "For we are consumed by thy anger; by thy wrath we are overwhelmed. Thou hast set our iniquities before thee, our secret sins in the light of thy countenance. For all our days pass away under thy wrath, and our years come to an end like a sigh" (Ps. XC.7-9). Dying and having to go is merely the reverse of being born. Death sees to the clearance job which is necessary so that room may be made in the limited space of this world for future generations. This becomes evident to us when we see that the nuptial flight of the day-flies is at the same time their death flight, and after that the mating of the queen-bee the drone drops dead on the ground. We therefore cannot

abstract death from the organic development of life without
undoing its entire structure.

We can go even further here and say that according to Ps. xc
we men experience in death only a particularly impressive
form of the fundamental transience, the continual being carried
away by the current of time which belongs to the essence of
the entire empirical world. When it is said: "The wages of sin
is death," then not merely one trait of the picture of the world
but its entire form of existence is thereby immediately connected with guilt. Consequently if we take this point of view
we can no longer, as in the first case, regard the world in which
we live and work as sacred and virgin territory, come forth
pure from God's creative hand. On the contrary at any time
the shadow of guilt has already fallen on this world and partly
determined the form of its existence and all the ordinances of
its life. That is why we can no longer say an unqualified "yes"
to this world.

These are the two points of view which have been contrasting
each other in ever sharper conflict, especially in the struggle
with the national-socialist conception of blood and soil. We
must therefore conscientiously go into this question: if we want
to abide by the direction which Jesus shows us, then which
decision must we take in the conflict between the two views?
If we want to answer the question according to the mind of
Jesus, we must keep in mind both:

(1) that the satanic character of our enmity towards God
must be given full emphasis. It must remain inexcusable, it
must not be explained by anything apart from itself, and

(2) that we must not attempt to harmonise by some kind of
synthetic view the contradiction which can be borne only in
faith, between the two comprehensive views, which necessarily
arises if we want to exercise the reality of the satanic without
losing sight of the reality of God. We must always say on the
one hand, "the devil is God's devil" – God is the sole agent in
Satan too. But on the other hand God is in no way responsible
for the rebellion against Himself; the fault lies only with us,
with the beings in which the will that is hostile to God is alive.

We shall try to give full value to each of these two views:

1. Our guilt before God is guilt only if we cannot in any way
explain and excuse it by the condition of the world in which

we were born or because of the environment in which we grew up. This excuse at once exists, if the biological structure of our organic existence or the temporal fundamental form of the reality to which we belong is impure in itself. Then we are excused in respect of our being far from God. Then we are already stained by the fact that our feet touch the soil of this earth and that to form "the work of our hands" we handle its dust. Thereby the guilt of our being far from God is taken from us. We are then excused by the conditions in which we were born and which defile us as soon as we touch them. The *original* sin of our enmity to God retains its inexcusable character if we have to say that conditions of life, forms of existence, biological ordinances can never be unclean in themselves. They can never as such carry a sin within themselves. The fault can always only be with myself who live under those conditions. Guilt is never something produced by circumstances, but always only something between God and myself. If guilt is to be found only in the sphere of the *original* relationship between Creator and creature, then the world, regarded apart from this relationship, is pure and innocent. We may therefore make the entirely unqualified statement: "Every thing created by God is good, and nothing is to be rejected" (1 Tim. IV.4); "all things are lawful" (1 Cor. VI.12); "all things are yours" (1 Cor. III.21).

We must first of all consider these unqualified statements by themselves and think them through to the end, although to Paul they are merely the protasis to a concluding sentence in which the disciple's obligation to Christ receives full weight ("and you are Christ's"). We can speak about the instructions which Jesus gives His disciples in a later context, when we are dealing with the question of the ethical task which Jesus allots to His Church. So for the time being we speak only of the protasis with which the Apostle begins.

What is the meaning of the universal statement contained in this protasis? Let us try to develop it. If something draws me away from God, something that belongs to this created world, e.g. the fine human body which sexually enraptures me, the riches to which my heart cleaves, or the worldly power that intoxicates me, then in all these cases what separates me from God is in reality not this object or this content of the world in itself. What inwardly defiles me can always only be the will of my own heart, which is hostile to God and which exists independently of the conditions of the world in which I live.

That is what Jesus means when He says in his sermon on the Jewish law of purity: "Not what goes into the mouth defiles a man, but what comes out of the mouth, this defiles a man" (Mt. xv.11). The anti-godly inclination which comes from the heart attempts to abuse all that God gives me as an instrument of demoniacal rebellion against God. If this hostile movement of our hearts were checked, if we were as God wants us to be, then all that now defiles us would lose its demoniacal character and be to us God's pure creation. Therefore the thesis holds good to the full extent: "to the pure all things are pure" (R.S.V.: "Everything is indeed clean", Rom. xiv.20). If we really remain in God, and God in us – supposing we were capable of that – then we have "the innocence of the senses". The sexual act as such is pure and sacred. Even the dirtiest book, the dirtiest play or film could not defile us, if we were really wholly close to God. For impurity can never be in the object as such, it is always in us, i.e. in the relation in which we are to God while dealing with the object in question. We always become unclean only through what happens between God and ourselves while we are reading the book or seeing the picture or while the play is being acted on the stage before our eyes.

If our heart is with God while we are watching the object, then we can see it with pure childish eyes. Then all that we experience, do and suffer is in the light of fellowship with God. Under this condition, and only under this condition, which in the world as it is has never come true except in the sinless life of Jesus, can we make the following statements: time is an expression of the kindness, patience and forbearance of God who gives us an opportunity for repentance. That the direction of time cannot be reversed is an expression of God's seriousness and urges us to make the best use of time. That we are carried away as a flood and are like the grass that flowers in the morning and soon withers, that is an ordering to which we submit with pleasure. For God is the only One who matters to us. It pleases us to wither so that God remains the One who alone has immortality (1 Tim. vi.16). With gladness therefore we say of all the things in this world which please us for a while:

"They all wear out like a garment . . . but thou art the same, and thy years have no end" (Ps. cii.26-7).

According to 1 Cor. xv the Creator has given to every creature the kind of body that He wished to give it. "All flesh is not alike" (v. 39), but the fundamental law of the divine creative order applies to every kind of body: "What is sown is perishable" (v. 42). Therefore if we are in a real relationship to Christ, then our grateful "yes" holds good in respect of death as well. "If we die, we die to the Lord" (Rom. xiv.8). We gratefully return to the Creator the existence which He entrusted to us for a certain time. Speaking of the death he expected to suffer in the service of the Church, Paul says: "Even if I am to be poured as a libation upon the sacrificial offering of your faith, I am glad and rejoice with you all. Likewise you also should be glad and rejoice with me" (Phil. ii.17-18). Dying thus becomes a service of God, an act of surrender to the Creator. When we die the blood of the sacrificial victim is poured out. We die for God. God takes back the life that He has given us, as our sacrifice of thanks. We gladly give up the place which we have so far occupied and in which we have worked, so that there may be room for others whom God has destined to something greater than us. Death will be the king of terror only as long as in selfish greed for life we resist the limit which God has set to our existence, in other words as long as we rebel against God. But if our mind rests in God's will, then we greet death as a welcome limitation of our individual existence by which room is made for God's new creation, without death thereby having the final say, and without, on the other hand, death thereby ceasing in this world of sin and death to be the "last enemy".

If in this sense we regard death as a divine regulation of creation, then we have also adopted a positive attitude to the fundamental law of organic life as a decree of God, according to which life can flourish only through the killing of life. In the sexual act we beget life and therein obey the command of the Creator: "Be fruitful and multiply, and fill the earth" (Gen. 1.28). But as living creatures in this temporal world can only grow by displacing and killing other living creatures, the necessity of killing is included in the command of fertility. As the act of procreation is sacred if therein we remain in commun-

ion with God, therefore it must also be possible to kill with a
pure heart – provided that we are at all able to remain with
God and to love Him above all things. In Rom. xiii.6 the
bearers of judicial power are called God's priests (λειτουργοί;
R.S.V. "ministers"). It is expressly stated that they carry the
sword, in other words that they are responsible for executions
(v. 4). According to that it may be regarded as possible that
men in a priestly attitude can kill other men without falling
away from fellowship with God. If therefore people kill with
an unclean heart, for lust of vengeance, hatred or rage, then
this is not because killing is in itself unclean. It should be possible for killing to be service of God, just as the death and fall
of the victim can be service of God. If this is not the case then
this can only be because the man who carries the sword, while
killing, leaves fellowship with God and becomes a victim of
the demons of hatred.

Consequently if a man really remains in the communion
with God for which he is destined, then in fact, as Walter
Künneth, agreeing with Kierkegaard, says, he can reach an
all-round positive attitude to the world: "Then he may . . . do
his work, enjoying his work, love his wife, enjoying his wife,
bring up his children for joy, love his fellow-men and enjoy
life." "The birds on the tree, the lily in the field, the deer in
the wood, the fish in the sea, countless multitudes of people
shout with joy: God is love. But so to speak as a foundation,
as the bass voice under all these sopranos sounds the *De profundis* of those who have been sacrificed: God is love."[1]

If transience, sexuality, strife for existence, having to kill,
dying and being sacrificed are ordinances in which we recognise God's government, then thereby, regarded more deeply,
the entire polar form of the empirical world in which we live
has been placed under the divine "yes". For the temporal
form, as shown in Vol. I, is the polar either-or relationship
between becoming and having become, between the non-
objective universal state of now, in which everything is as yet
undecided, and the decided unchangeable state of objectivity
into which all that happens changes continually. If I am with
God, then the deciding character of my existence is the glorious
possibility of making the decision for God from moment to

[1] Walter Künneth.

moment anew. The order of the strife for existence, of killing and having to die is the expression of the polar relationship between "I" and "thou", discussed in Vol. I. For the thou-relation is the logically insoluble high tension which comes into being through the either-or relationship between two mutually exclusive claims.

The singular belongs to the essence of "I". Thou and I both have to claim the same place from which everything else becomes "not-I". This polarity expresses itself in a well-known biological fact: in every organic structure there is an impulse to spread indefinitely and to reproduce infinitely. And all the same the process of life is kept going only as long as this unlimited impulse is checked by other organisms which resist it because they have the same unlimited impulse, as a fire burns only as long as there is unburned material left. As long as there is life there must be this polar tension between the vital claims of various living beings. The whole history of organic life, and also the history of states, is kept moving only through this unlimited but ever inhibited impulse for power and world-conquest. Life would at once come to a standstill if this un-limited impulse were not there or if there were no resistance for it to overcome. If therefore the strife for existence, killing and dying are sacred ordinances of creation to him who remains in God, then there is a divine "yes" to the polar form of existence in which we live, to the relation of contents and the relationship of spaces, the structure of which we discussed in Vol. I.

2. Consequently this sacredness of creation and all its ordinances comes into force only for him who is in communion with God. The more we approach the condition of love of God, the more the veil lifts from our eyes and the glory of the order of creation dawns on us. The further we move away from this condition and lose our connexion with God, the more our eyes are veiled and a vague and incoherent picture stands before our eyes. We see organic structures in senseless vital impulses striving for the infinite and tearing each other to pieces with terrible tortures.

From this one could draw the conclusion that it is only because of our clouded eye that we are not able to see God's world in its pure shine. Creation as such is not affected by this fact. Of creation as it is in itself what is said at the end of the story of the divine creation remains as true as ever: "And God saw every thing that he had made, and behold, it was very good" (Gen. 1.31). We could draw this conclusion only if the Platonic view were right, according to which "I" and the world exist independently of each other. According to Plato the ego stays in the world only for the time being, as though in an inn, to leave it again and to work itself up into a higher region. Therefore the fate of the world can be indifferent to me if I have saved my soul in a better beyond. If this were true, then the ego and the world which it has before its eyes could be separated, as one can separate a table and the lamp on top of it. No change occurs in the table, whether the lamp is burning more or less clearly. Similarly the world would be just as pure and valuable, even though the veiled eyes of sinful man could only see it in semi-darkness.

This view becomes untenable if the relation between "I" and the world is different from what is assumed in Platonic philosophy. If the dynamic philosophy developed in Vol. I is right, then "I" and the world belong together in an inseparable unity. "I" and "it" is the same relation, seen from another point of view, like becoming and having become. As a willing and knowing ego I belong entirely inside the world's state of becoming. I cannot save myself by jumping out of the world and sending it flying behind me into nothingness. My destiny and its destiny belong together. There is no world without an ego, nor an ego without the world. Existence always means "to be in the world".[2] But if "I" and the world form an inseparable unity, then therein the world has been drawn into the insoluble contradiction which is given in the fact that we participate in a satanic rebellion against God. The shadow of *original* sin, which comes between "I" and God is cast on the world and all its ordinances too.

[2] Heidegger.

CHAPTER 15

The Contradiction between the two Comprehensive Views of the World

How far does the *original* sin which separates us from God cast a shadow also on the world to the shaping of which we contribute? If under the guidance of Jesus we want to take the reality of the satanic into account, then a high tension comes into being between two comprehensive views which to our thinking are incompatible and only form an incomprehensible unity to faith; that is, the view of God's sole agency and the view of a conflict in which God is at war with an opposing power. This contradiction applies first of all to the *original* relation between God and "I". What follows for the world, which under our responsible co-influence is changing all the time from the undecided into the decided condition? Here too a contradiction must arise between two incompatible comprehensive views.

In its present form this world carries two possibilities which contradict each other and nevertheless are both there. The first possibility corresponds with the comprehensive view of God's sole agency. It comes into force if the ego that has its position in the midst of the world at the same time entirely rests in God. For this ego, resting in God, everything, including sexual life, the life-and-death struggle between creatures, killing and having to die, is a decree of God who works all in all. But then our will does not rest in God as it should. Of course we can only state this as a fact and expect everyone who is honest with himself to admit it. We cannot demonstrate this statement. To achieve that we would have to organise a general inquiry with all people who have ever lived and will ever live. Although such a demonstration is not possible, we yet make this statement in the very definite expectation that all men who know their own hearts will agree. None of us men is so near to God that he could really apprehend the sole agency of God in all that is and happens. We can speak about it in words; but unless a miracle happens to us we can only for moments adopt the attitude towards the world which would follow from this statement. And we fail in particular really to hold on to this in the critical situations in which it should be shown whether we really are able to praise God with all our heart for all that He does.

At normal times, when pleasure and pain, happiness and suffering in our life remain within moderate limits, we may perhaps be able to accept the destiny of our lives altogether from God's hand. Whether the gratitude which in those cases we express to God is genuine, whether we really want only what God wills, will only be shown in cases which the New Testament calls temptations, in which faith is tested for genuineness like gold in the fire. This happens when the measure of happiness and suffering is exceeded one way or the other, either when the fortune that comes to us, the power which we gather in our hands, reaches an excess that disturbs our inner balance, or when the grief which crushes us, the sacrifice demanded of us seems so senseless that it is impossible for us to harmonise it with God's love. In these two cases it is quite clear to us, that even superabundant happiness should not for a moment tempt us to become possessed by a selfish lust for happiness and power and to lose God in the process. We should be so united with God, that even under a fatal blow, in which we simply cannot discover any meaning, we can, according to Kierkegaard's word, with all our heart sing the *De Profundis* of the victims: God is love. But we must honestly confess that if our trust in God is put to these severe tests, then in most cases we are instantly thrown out of the position which we should have held, and we only pull ourselves together when we rally our scattered forces and attempt to reconquer the lost fortress.

Luther says in his rough German honesty, one cannot pray in the nuptial bed. When the transport of erotic joy reaches a certain climax, then we weak men lose contact with God, not because it is in itself impossible even at the heights of happiness blessedly to rest in God but simply because our strength of prayer fails. After a serious mining accident the first effect on those who stand in the mortuary where hundreds of fine men are lying dead, and hear the heart-breaking crying of the wives and children who have been robbed of their bread-winners, is despair, rebellion and hostility towards their fate. Only after some time, maybe, the crushed trust in God gradually rises again and we are able to say "Yet I am always with Thee".

Think for instance, to take an example from life, of the accident that happened some years ago in a city in central Germany. Four children, girls between eight and nine years of age, were playing at the bottom of a large trunk which they used as a doll's house, and were suffocated when the heavy lid fell and locked itself after they had gone in. When the trunk was opened, the doctor stated that the children could have been saved if someone had arrived ten minutes earlier. It is possible that afterwards the mothers of the children eventually understood that the law of gravity according to which the lid had to fall at that unfortunate moment is a sacred ordinance of God's creation without which the world could not even exist, and that the accident that took away their children was a trial through which God wanted to purify them. But under the deadening first blow of such an event there is no one among us who is immediately capable of this attitude. As long as we are concerned with the case in theory only it is clear to us that our will should rest in God's will in such a manner that we can calmly and trustfully, without any defensive movement, accept such a blow which destroys our happiness in life, in the certainty that it comes from Him who loves us. But if the thing becomes practical and the blow really hits ourselves, then we are at first thrown out of our attitude of trust and we clench our fist in wild rebellion against the power that destroys our life.

In all cases of this kind it is evident that the bridge that leads us to God holds only as long as it need not carry too heavy a load. As soon as too heavy a train goes over it, as soon as there is an overweight of pleasure or pain, the bridge collapses. But if we are so unable to stand the test which, according to the New Testament, tries the genuineness of our faith as gold is tried by fire, then the suspicion arises that the praise of God and the gratitude for the order of His creation of which we are capable at quiet times of normal burden may perhaps only be due to God's guidance not being too much in contrast to what we ourselves wish and need.

We see that the world in its present form, it is true, does carry with it the first possibility, the standpoint of God's sole agency. It can be experienced as a sacred ordinance of God's creation. However, as within us there is a will which is hostile to God, we may know about this first possibility but it remains beyond our reach. As long as the pure relationship to God has not been restored, the second possibility, the standpoint of conflict, is ever in force with us. The same ordinances which seen by the pure eye of trust in God are God's sacred ordinances, become demoniacal powers and instruments of rebellion against God as soon as we regard them with the clouded eye of man estranged from God.

To the man united with God the polar relationship between "I" and "thou", through which alone my world is immediately accessible to me while the world of the other man remains closed to me, is the great opportunity of love, in which he sacrifices himself – whom he knows – for the sake of another who is a stranger to him. To the man who is estranged from God the same relationship between "I" and "thou" is the great temptation to say: "The skin is nearer than the shirt," "Am I my brother's keeper?" and coldly and mercilessly to disregard the need of the other, like the priest and the Levite. To the will that is concentrated on God the deciding character of our actions, which is due to the temporal form of our existence, is the glorious opportunity to decide for God from moment to moment. But in the state of being far from God my subjective power of decision is the great temptation to decide against God in Promethean defiance and demoniacal autonomy, as the ego that is proud of its own liberty. The joy of the world which in a normal state inclines me to gratitude to God becomes in the state of being far from God the insatiable greed that drags me away from Him. But suffering and death cause fear and despair and quarrelling with God.

If we consider the relationship between God and the world from this point of view then we arrive at the standpoint of conflict, no longer kept in balance by the standpoint of God's sole agency. For from this point of view we can think only of a God who wages war against opposing demoniacal powers which rebel against Him. God's government of the world then consists in permitting these hostile powers, and in superior governing wisdom using them to keep us, "the weak rebels" (Dostoevsky), in check. He allows the intoxication of power, the demoniacal greed of money and erotic passion to be aroused in us in order to steel our character by this fiery heat and to test us, whether we allow ourselves to be enslaved and to perish as slaves of our instincts or whether we are victorious in the struggle for our self-control. Death, which being far from God we fear, is the scourge with which God threatens us, His judgment on our guilt. In a world of men far from God it does in fact hold good: "The wages of sin is death." "His wrath causes us, so to perish."

In other words, there are two comprehensive views of reality which we are no longer able to harmonise reflectively and which nevertheless we have to take equally seriously if we want to do justice to the real condition of the world in which we live. Paul places the two pictures abruptly beside one another. In I Cor. xv.35ff, the transience is the Creator's ordinance for the present world. But in Rom. v and vi the transience is due to the reaction of God's wrath to man's *original* sin. The two standpoints which confront each other in the present dispute of the philosophies, the standpoint of the unqualified assertion of the world and the other standpoint in which the "yes" to the world is interrupted by a "no", are therefore, according to the Bible, not two standpoints between which we have to make a choice. Paradoxically they are both true at the same time and in their contrast give expression to the real state of affairs. For it is characteristic of this state of affairs that it cannot be expressed in one comprehensive view but only in two contradictory pictures which keep each other in balance.

We have already convinced ourselves that we can only bear the contradiction between the polar world and the supra-polar reality of the omnipresent God in the certainty that He will solve the high tension which we cannot solve ourselves. All genuine believers in God therefore can bear with life only in the glowing expectation of an ultimate condition in which God solves the contradiction, in which consequently He will be "all in all". It is in keeping with this that according to Luke's report Jesus says clearly in His dispute with the Sadducees that when the Kingdom of God comes in power, then the coherent fundamental ordinances of the polar world, sexuality and death, will both cease. "The sons of this age marry and are given in marriage; but those who are accounted worthy to attain to that age and to the resurrection from the dead neither marry nor are given in marriage, for they cannot die any more, because they are equal to angels and are sons of God, being sons of the resurrection" (Lk. xx.34-6). When therefore God is all in all, then the two things will no longer exist, which most of all have the power themselves of being both God's ordinances and diabolical instruments of Satan: the excess of joy brought forth by sex, which fills man estranged from God with a selfish ecstasy, and the excessive pain of death which fills him with terror and despair. When God is all in all, then the contradiction of the two comprehensive views will be done away with; a new form of the world will be substituted for the old form which carries the two possibilities with it, a new form in which there is only one possibility.

If with glowing expectation we look forward to the change of the world, then involuntarily the question arises: is there, corresponding to the end that Jesus promises, a beginning into which this end returns? Is the end the restoration of an *original* state which existed earlier? Was it through an accident that the world got into its present state out of which it has to lift itself if it is to return to the *original* state? According to the tradition which we have concerning Him, Jesus made no express statement on this question. It is true that the Old Testament, to which Jesus so often refers in his views, speaks of a satanic enticement, through which the first men fell in sin, and of their expulsion from paradise, though it gives us no clear picture of the change in the whole form of the world brought about by this fall. But if the disobedience of the first men entailed the fate of death (Gen. II.17) and the transience of man is an expression of God's judgment of wrath on our sin (Ps. xc.7-9), then this is clearly in line with later Judaism and with Paul's Epistle to the Romans, where death appears as the "wages of sin" (vi.23, cf. viii.20) and therefore as divine punishment inflicted on man. Jesus' exorcisms of demons too show one thing clearly: that the satanic power is the ultimate cause of guilt and that the world has not yet reached its final state because this power has not yet been vanquished. Certainly, we shall be ripe for the ultimate knowledge of this mystery only when the final victory has been gained. Until then we know these connexions only "in part" (1 Cor. XIII.12). Only then will our eyes be fully opened to the *origin* and meaning of God's creation.

K

PART FOUR

GOD'S REVELATION IN CHRIST

CHAPTER 16

The Incomprehensible Fact

L ET US STOP for a moment to clarify the conclusions we have
reached in the preceding sections and the task which we
still have in front of us.

We saw first of all that an understanding of what the Church
of Christ testifies concerning her Master depends on whether
we admit from our own experience that we are not able to
posit, choose, think or conclude from the empirical world the
reality which alone gives support to our soul, rest to our thinking and its sanction to our actions. We cannot understand the
attitude of the Early Church with its determined renunciation
of self-guidance as long as we believe, like the Idealists, that
the fact of our existence gives us access to the Absolute and
hence to a certitude of the right decisions in life and triumph
over pain and death. If we believe this, it is better for us not
to occupy ourselves with the faith of this Church at all. We
can only misunderstand it because we are not yet aware of the
universal distressed condition of man which Christ has come to
cure. "Those who are well have no need of a physician"
(Mk. ii.17). The message that God has given us a Leader to
whom we can cleave in the ultimate question of life, concerns
only the limited circle of people who by painful experiences
have come to realise that we cannot by our own thought and
will break through the curse of the polar relations in which we
are enclosed. We can, it is true, speak the lofty words which
form the crowning end of all human philosophy: "the Absolute",
"the unqualified", "the *origin*". But these words are to our
mind merely symbols for unsolved questions or ungratified
needs, not realities which we can grasp. Therefore these words
give no strength in life and no comfort in death.

Corresponding with the polar character of our knowledge is
the state of being far from God with which our whole existence
is burdened, the incomprehensible uncertainty and the unin-

telligibility of the omnipresent ultimate Reality, the universal human need of seeking the lost way home by prayer and exercises of concentration and forms of worship, the Hamlet-like indecision from which we suffer in connexion with all our everyday decisions, the fear of suffering in the world and the terror of death. He who has not experienced this condition has as yet no soil in which the seed of the testimony concerning Christ can fall. He still belongs to the "well" who do not need the physician.

But as soon as we have realised the absurd situation of man, there are two possibilities left for us. The first possibility is to regard the situation as desperate. Then we no longer expect any help but settle ourselves within our human possibilities. We can then either raise a given reality of this polar world by our own choice and decision to the rank of the absolute because neither as individuals nor as a nation can we live and work without an *original* substance. Or we can follow the alternative course of entering on the way of mysticism, and seek for rest in the point of indifference beyond all polar contrasts. But in choosing either of these ways we remain within the limits set by the fundamental structure of the world that is at our disposal.

However there is another possibility. That is the belief that beyond all that we ourselves can think or infer there is a guidance that opens to us the door to the ultimate Reality, a Power which delivers us from the distressed condition in which we can only choose one of the two ways mentioned above.

If the Early Church is right in saying that we have been given a Leader who has authority, then the existence of this unique Figure in the midst of a puzzling world is the precious treasury and the living source from which we can draw all that we can know concerning the ultimate question. Even if this consists only of fragments which in no way satisfy our need of a comprehensive philosophy but leave unsolved many questions asked by our thirst of knowledge, yet the gathering of those fragments is far more important and valuable than the most ingenious and brilliant systems of thought which we have thought out for ourselves. In the same way, if we want to know something about the first ascent of a mountain peak, the incomplete and fragmentary report of a simple mountain-guide who survived a fatal accident during the expedition is infinitely more valuable than the thrilling presentation by a great poet who has pictured the adventure only in his poetic imagination. For the important thing to us in this vital question is not a comprehensive system or an aesthetically satisfactory overall picture. The question on which our eternal destiny depends is too serious for that. The only thing that matters is whether the little that we can know really does come from the authority which cannot only utter guesses concerning the ultimate things, as all human thinkers and poets do, but has God's mandate to instruct us on them.

In our argument so far we have ventured to base ourselves on the confidence that God has actually placed the guidance of mankind as regards the ultimate question in the hands of the One who meets our eyes in the New Testament. We have therefore put aside any thoughts of our own and directed all our attention to the precious and unfathomable reality which encounters us in the Christ of the Gospels. For our reflexion too we have accepted His guidance and have set ourselves the one task of exhausting the content of this unfathomable reality. In the questions which weigh upon our hearts we have addressed ourselves to the one authority from which we expect valid answers. In so doing we have moved from the peripheric to the intrinsic. We have first asked the general question: quite irrespective of who the Leader is and what He tells us, what does it mean for the understanding of our whole human situation, that we have been given a Leader? It means, as we saw, that all our attempts to guide ourselves in the ultimate question are vain and that therefore we live in a condition of being far from God. From this the second question followed as a matter of course: what is the deepest reason for this being far from God? The answer that Jesus gave to this question was found in the fact that all His life he reckoned with an invisible enemy which arises against God. By the fact that this will of enmity against God exists, a contradiction which we cannot solve has been introduced into everything that we can say about God.

From the answers which we have received on these two first questions a third fundamental question arises, about which we shall still have to speak before we can meditate on the concrete full content of the figure of Christ. We have to ask: if the reality of which we are part contains a twofold possibility and is therefore simultaneously in God's omnipresence and in guilty remoteness from God, how then is it at all possible that in the midst of this empirical world there should be a place where we can receive instruction and guidance as regards the absolute Reality? How can absolute guidance come into force within a world in which all things mutually condition each other? These two things seem to be contradictory: belief in the figure of a Leader who stands right in the midst of this world and has absolute authority, and what we learn about the form of the world as soon as we accept His leadership.

It is no use seeking an answer to this question by our own reflexion, e.g. by starting from the dialectic relation between the Infinite and the finite, between the Absolute and the relative, between Eternity and time, and meditating on how through the Infinite becoming finite, the Absolute becoming relative and Eternity becoming time the contradiction between the Divine and the demoniacal could be solved. All these profound speculations do not get us even one step beyond the polar thinking of which alone we are capable. If there is any possibility at all of breaking through the curse of polarity it can only be one which we cannot think out in view of our form of existence, but only accept. We can therefore only answer the question how an absolute Leader's authority can come into force in the world of relativities in which we live, if we look upon the inexhaustible fact itself that envelops us when we read the New Testament.

The collection of reports, epistles and prophecies which we have before us in the New Testament is not a philosophical tract like Marcus Aurelius' *Meditations*, neither is it a collection of moral proverbs like the discourses of *Kung Fu-tse* (*Lun Yu*); nor are they the kind of legends of saints to illustrate a certain ideal of piety that we find in Buddhist literature. Rather is this collection from beginning to end the outcome of the inner emotion caused by an unbelievable event. The Gospel according to Mark, which according to many scholars is the oldest report we have and which according to tradition we owe to Peter's interpreter in whose parents' house some of the events had taken place, reads even now like the brief report of a messenger who records without commentary or reflexion an

event which has strongly moved him; while by the characteristic εὐθύς ("immediately") he hurries from one point to the
other until the terrible end. The forerunner who announces
that which is to come, Elijah who was sent "before the great
and terrible day of Jahveh comes" (Mal. iv.5), already speaks
with the visionary excitement roused by a catastrophe which
casts its shadow into the future: "Even now the axe is laid to
the root of the trees." That is to say: an event is approaching
under the mighty blows of which oaks will fall. "You brood
of vipers! who warned you to flee from the wrath to come?
Bear fruit that befits repentance" (Mt. iii.7-10). And now, as
the event itself approaches, the news that that which has been
expected for centuries has come spreads like wild-fire from one
person to another. Andrew "first found his brother Simon and
said to him, 'We have found the Messiah'". Philip finds
Nathanael and says to him: "We have found him of whom
Moses in the law and also the prophets wrote, Jesus of Nazareth,
the son of Joseph" (Jn. 1.41, 45).

The mixture of joy and fear at an unheard-of event produced
in the Gospels a new form of literature. Even their style is
different from that of a writer seeing an event in historical
perspective and trying to produce an unimpeachable account.
It is rather the way in which a messenger gives a report of an
event to people whose destiny depends on it. In this manner,
for example, a shipwrecked man who has come to land safely
tells the relations of those who have been lost about the storm.
At such a moment there is no point in drawing stirring pictures
with an epic sweep. There is no time for that now. The important thing is to tell the people whose lives are so strongly
affected, only what is relevant, but to do this so clearly that
they get an accurate picture. That is why the last days of the
life of Jesus, in which the important decisions are made,
receive relatively much more space than everything earlier.

Clemens Alexandrinus[1] gives a note on the origin of what is
perhaps the oldest Gospel, which is so contrary to traditional
views, that it may well be based on a correct recollection. He
says that people who had heard Peter asked Mark, who remem-
bered Peter's words particularly clearly, to write down his
recollections and pass them on. "When Peter heard this, he

---

[1] *Hypotyposes*, in Eusebius, *Hist. Ecc.*, vi, xiv.6, Migne, *P.G.* vol. 20, p. 552.

neither publicly opposed nor supported it." The rock-apostle, on whom Jesus wanted to build the Church, evidently did not set great store by having memories of the great events put down in writing. Maybe he believed that the end of the world was so near that it was no longer worth while writing books. If it had been a matter of philosophical principles or moral maxims, then codification would have been most essential. But here the all-important thing was to keep the memory of an event alive. And to Peter it seemed more important to do so by the living word of the eye-witnesses than by writing it down.

From all this one can see that the aim of the witnesses speaking and reporting in the New Testament, is not to convince their readers of a general truth or of the validity of a certain morality. They do not wish, like those who told the Buddhist legends, to illustrate the "sacred truth of suffering and the elimination of suffering" by examples from the life of a master. They want to bear witness to an event which happened at this single point of time and which once and for all changed the whole face of the earth, the entire relationship between time and Eternity.

The Epistle to the Hebrews compares this once-and-for-all character which this event has for the whole world to the once-and-for-all character which death has for the existence of the individual. "And just as it is appointed for men to die once, and after that comes judgment, so Christ, having been offered once . . ." (Heb. IX.27-8). In these and the preceding verses the word $\dot{a}\pi a\xi$ (once) occurs three times to characterise the event. The same is meant by 1 Pet. III.18: "Christ also died for sins once," and Rom. VI.10: "The death he died he died to sin once for all ($\dot{\epsilon}\phi\dot{a}\pi a\xi$)."

What was this unique event, which according to all these witnesses is a fact that changes the situation of the world once and for all, a fact that we can grasp only gradually and step by step, by moving from the peripheric to the intrinsic, from the general meaning of the event to its inner meaning? At first it is announced by the general statement, "The kingdom of God is at hand" (Mk. 1.15). Before this Christ coming out of the water saw "the heavens opened" ($\sigma\chi\iota\zeta o\mu\dot{\epsilon}\nu o\upsilon s$ $\tau o\dot{\upsilon}s$ $o\dot{\upsilon}\rho a\nu o\dot{\upsilon}s$, Mk. 1.10). The sphere of the transcendent, long closed, has opened. The silence of God which has weighed on the centuries like a leaden sky since the last prophets stopped speaking, has ceased. Now "the time is fulfilled, the hour has come". The New Testament calls what has happened here, a *"being given"* for which one can never be sufficiently grateful (χάρις, χαρισθῆναι), and also a salvation (σωτηρία), i.e. a rescue from otherwise certain drowning.

All these words are meaningful only if at all times, even when the life-boat has saved us, we are conscious of the other terrible possibility which might equally well have come true, indeed which would have been infinitely more likely. Heaven might have remained closed. We might have perished in the unfilled vacuum of the unsolved question. Only if we feel the weight of divine silence which no man can break in exactly the same way as those who were "looking forward to the consolation of Israel", can we hear what the witnesses report exactly as it should be heard, i.e. "with fear and great joy", in the attitude of men whose lives depend on whether all this is merely a dream – whether even now mankind, like a victim of a mountain-accident in his feverish delirium, is mistaking the beat of its own heart for the approach of the rescue party – or whether the event, the approach of which the combined longing of all mankind had not been able to hasten on, has really come: the event of events, the approach of the Kingdom of Heaven.

We men of our time are probably nearer again to the situation in which the first messengers took up the message of the day of the Messiah than the people of any of the intervening centuries. "At no other time has the world realised in itself the existence of such yawning emptiness, of such an abyss in which everything has to be swallowed up. The same labour-pains of those days are suddenly occurring again; there is the same voice of the preacher in the wilderness, heard by no one: 'Prepare the way of the Lord.' The same axe is still lying by the roots of the tree; the same invisible snares are covering the world; there is the same thief coming in the night – the last judgment; there is the same word written in the same fiery lettering against a sky black with thunder and becoming ever darker and more threatening: 'The End'."[2]

[2] Merezhkovsky.

CHAPTER 17

God Has Spoken

IN WHAT we have said so far we have merely described the outer circle within which the event to be grasped is to be found. The ultimate question has found an answer. The Kingdom of Heaven, the sphere which lies in the other direction which we cannot reach, has come noticeably near to our ungodly reality. But how has that happened? Wherein consists that unique event by which the time was fulfilled? If we want to grasp an event we have to give up any attempts to think it out or to construe it beforehand by the aid of our own thoughts and concepts. As soon as we try to deduce what has happened from a general principle which we already have, we are no longer capable of seeing the event itself in its newness and mystery. Therefore our thinking cannot start until we have received the news of the event. Our reflexion can only copy what we have been mysteriously granted.

Let us first of all listen to what the messengers say. Their first and most general statement about the event which fills time with an eternal content is this: God has spoken. "In many and various ways God spoke of old to our fathers by the prophets; but in these last days he has spoken to us by a Son" (Heb. 1.1-2). That does not merely mean that this event was accompanied by words, i.e. by instructions, exhortations and announcements. No, the whole event must be summed up to the effect that in it God Himself took on words, in other words that in it God's Word became flesh. For the moment let us disregard the content of God's speech, and limit ourselves to the general statement: the event that filled time with Eternity took place in the form of talking, that is to say in the form which in conversation between "I" and "thou" we call speaking and listening. Let us try to delineate reflectingly what that means.

If we should try to form a conception of what would happen

if God were to abandon His mystery and come into the open, on the basis of the idea of the quest for the unknown God, the whole discussion in the previous chapter shows that we could only picture it as the dissolution of the entire present state of the world. For the state of the world always bears within itself the twofold possibility that it can always be both God's creation and an instrument of satanic rebellion against Him. It can be experienced as God's sole agency and as the battleground of conflicting powers. If the Absolute is to come forth from its invisibility and its mystery there seems to be only one possible way: the whole first created world in which we live, the form of which is partly determined by the existence of the opposing satanic will, must be dissolved. Satanism must be destroyed and from the flames in which Satan perishes a new pure creation must arise in which "God is all in all" (1 Cor. xv.28, "everything to everybody", R.S.V.), a new universal condition of which it can be said: "Now the salvation and the power and the kingdom of our God . . . have come" (Rev. xii.10). Now God Himself becomes the sun, that is to say the source of light by which everything is illuminated and flooded with light (Rev. xxi.23, xxii.5). This dissolution of the first form of the world by a new creation which is no longer in the shadow of the satanic would, according to our human way of thinking, be the only possible way for God to come into the open. But the New Testament witnesses mention this possibility only in the second place. The first thing that they report is something quite different, something that would never have occurred to a human mind: God has not destroyed this world of which Satan is the prince. He has established a contact with it, and that in the form which between man and man we call "speaking". God has spoken. What does that mean?

As long as the essence of transcendence has not dawned on us, as long as we still conceive of the beyond in a pre-Copernican manner, as something in space, as a higher sphere above the limited universe, we can always conceive of the intercourse between God and ourselves only to the effect that the ceiling of the lower space in which we live is suddenly opened and through the opening something comes down from the upper world into the world below. The heavens are rent. We see the heavens "opened". A ray of light breaks like the sun through broken clouds or a being from the supra-terrestrial world comes down and either changes into an earthly being, e.g. an animal, as depicted in Ovid's *Metamorphoses* or moves about in human form like Odin the wanderer with the cloud-hat.

But as soon as we have realised that this empirical world in which we find ourselves is an infinity, complete in itself, all these conceptions instantly become impossible and can henceforth be used only as inadequate figurative speech. An opening in the ceiling, a window or a door leading from this space to another space is inconceivable. Anything that occurs within the sphere of this world is part of this infinity which is complete in itself. Is it then at all conceivable, is it not *a priori* impossible that within this infinity the manifestation should take place of something that is not of this world?

The apostles of Jesus Christ testify that incomprehensibly God has made such a thing possible. They also give us a starting point for an understanding of this divine act. They compare it with the way in which within the polar world two unlimited spaces meet, and more precisely with the form in which "I" and "thou" encounter one another in conversation. It is *a priori* evident that this comparison does not explain the miracle to which the apostles testify, or make it comprehensible to us. For we are dealing here with a relation between the world of relativities, the only world we can comprehend, and the absolute, supra-polar *original* Being that is closed to us. As the essence of this *original* Reality is inscrutable and unfathomable to our cognition, any relation to the empirical world into which it can enter is also incomprehensible. All that we are told about this relation therefore can *a priori* only mean that a mystery beyond our thinking is here expressed in a form adapted to our human comprehension. This gives extra value to any suggestion made by the men authorised to proclaim the mystery by Christ Himself. We must take full advantage of all that they tell us on the subject and exhaust it in every respect.

What does it mean, when the witnesses of the fact of salvation say that this event is not merely accompanied by words of God, but in its full content is "the Word of God", the form in which God speaks? What does it mean, for example, when the Seer of the Revelation sees the figure of Christ with eyes like flames, arrayed in a garment sprinkled with blood "and the name by which he is called is The Word of God" (Rev. xix.12-13)? To exhaust the full meaning of this we have to remember what speaking is, as set out in Volume I.[1] Let us once more briefly recall what we had to say there about the essence of the word.

1. According to its true essence the word is not an object but an act, that is to say the act which takes place when I hear what you say or when you hear what I say. As an object the word does not differ from other sounds which reach my ear. Only by the act of hearing does this one sound separate itself as something different and unique in the sea of sounds around me and become a word.

2. The peculiar thing about the sound of a word, which distinguishes it from all other sounds, is that in the hearing of this sound an encounter is effected between you and me. I hear the word that you speak. I speak the word that you hear. We meet one another because I know that speaking on your part and hearing on my part are the same act. In speaking and hearing therefore there is something common to you and to me, to the world of your consciousness and to the world of my consciousness, though these worlds are altogether inaccessible to each other. I cannot look into you and you cannot look into me. That is the only reason why words are necessary between us. If we were open to one another, the thing for which all lovers long, then words between us would cease immediately. We would silently be open to one another. All speaking would have become superfluous.

The word therefore creates a point of identity between two spaces of consciousness which are outside one another, which even while speaking remain foreign and ulterior to one another. In *God Transcendent* we called this unity within a contrast that cannot be done away with, a meeting between spaces infinite in themselves as distinguished from the boundary between limited spaces, e.g. between the black and white squares on a chessboard or between adjoining rooms in a house. Two areas which touch each other limit one another. Two spaces which meet each other retain their infinity. They pass through one another. That is how two infinite lines intersect at one point. Two infinite planes have one secant. In the same

[1] *God Transcendent* (pp. 168ff).

manner two spaces of consciousness remain infinities in themselves, while the word is a point of unity between them.

3. This meeting between two spaces which remain ulterior
to each other can take place – this is the third thing important
for the essence of the word – only if there is a comprehending
space in which the two spaces are co-ordinated and to which
they are subordinated. Lines intersect only within a plane.
Planes can intersect only within three-dimensional space. Here
comes into force the dimensional part-relationship between
infinite spaces which is to be distinguished from the quantitative part-relationship between limited objects, e.g. the
bricks of a wall or the notes of a melody. Consequently no
meeting can take place between the comprehending space and
the subordinate spaces co-ordinated within it, e.g. between
three-dimensional space and a plane which forms part of it.
A meeting is possible only between two spaces which are co-
ordinated because they are both terms of the same comprehending space within which they meet each other, that is to
say between line and line, plane and plane. In the same way
you and I can meet each other in words only if we enter into
the same level, more precisely if we are co-ordinated as terms
of a comprehending space within which the meeting takes
place. We have called the space within which you and I meet
the space within the "space" of the Present, and the space in
which your objective space and my objective space are co-
ordinated World-space (*Weltraum*, Universe).

4. By all this we have merely been speaking of what the
word has in common with all other meetings between spaces.
But what is peculiar to the word, what distinguishes the word
from all other meetings? In speaking I meet with a "thou".
I now experience the existence of the other one who speaks to
me, and who does this not in words alone. The first and most
elementary relation between me and the other one who is
"eternally foreign" to me is that in my attempt to shape the
world I meet with an opposing will that gets in my way and
wants to shape the world differently; and I become aware that
the activity of this other one causes me suffering, in my passion I
perceive his action. I therefore experience the existence of the
other one as the silent presence of a dynamic resistance which
is incomprehensible to me because it contradicts the decision

of my will. The existence of this silent opposing power is the condition of any speech between us. The word that you speak breaks the ban of your silent action and explains it to me. It tells me what you mean by it and what aim you have in view. It addresses itself to my will and tries to move me to decide for your aim. It endeavours to draw my resisting will in the direction of your action. As your and my existence consists in continual decisions to shape the world there can be no real speech between us in which there is no struggle about the future form of the world. There is no word which is not directly or indirectly concerned with quite concrete practical vital decisions.

We have thus made it clear in outline what speech means in the dealing of man with man. We can now gather what it means when the apostles say: God has spoken. There is not only the silent presence of Him who determines all things, the creative activity which we perceive at every point of the world "in vital energy, in the tempest of action", in the surf of the sea and the conflicts of nations. At a definite place God also exists in a second, completely different manner, viz. as the One who explains to us the meaning of this whole silent display of power. God speaks. What does that mean?

To answer this question we have to take full advantage of all that according to the foregoing belongs to the essence of speech, and first of all apply the three essential characteristics of speech explained above. In a further section we shall deal with a fourth characteristic.

When God speaks to us, then already by the fact that He deals with us in this manner He makes us realise in a humbling way that we are in an ungodly condition. For He comes to us in the way in which two spaces meet of which one is closed to the other. He comes to us indirectly, "from without", i.e. from outside the space in which we are comprehended, as one who from the outside knocks on the wall of my prison and thereby makes me painfully aware that I am in captivity. If God comes to us from without then thereby He makes us feel that we are outside Him. God's speech therefore is not merely grace and an incomprehensible gift but as such it is also judgment.

Therefore natural man involuntarily rebels against the Word of God, not only against its offensive content but also against the form of address as such. We sense that this form of self-revelation is not in accordance with the true relationship which should exist between God and ourselves. As long as we have not realised the ungodliness in which we live, as long as with the idealism of Mysticism we believe that we already are in the normal condition and that access to God is immediately open to us, it seems to us an insult to our human dignity, indeed a disparagement of the intrinsic essence of religion, that God should meet us as an ulterior authority with commandments and announcements. "I cannot possibly rate the word so highly."[2] The Word seems far too indirect for the communion which we should have with God. It seems to destroy the immediate relationship. It creates a wall between God and us, built with words for stones. "Woe, between us are words, mass and wall massively built. I cannot reach God through the word. Away from the word! Away from the house of sound!"[3]

That we instinctively reject the Word as the bridge between God and ourselves is not merely because like Faust in Martha's garden we want to substitute a sub-spiritual ecstasy for the consciously spiritual communion into which God wants to enter with us, or because we should like to eliminate the whole "I-thou" relationship between God and ourselves and extinguish ourselves. Certainly all the mystical religions of identity, because they desire to eliminate the "I-thou" relationship, at the same time also decline the word as an organ of revelation. So, for example, Japanese Zen-Buddhism eliminates from religion all that is written. Sacred writings are merely "the window through which we look at the great landscape of spiritual nature". But even where the "thou"-relationship between God and man is in full force, where any mystical fusion with the deity is rejected as paganism, as in the prophetic religion of ancient Israel, there still remains a clear feeling that instruction through the word, as possible in the present world, is yet an imperfect condition to be overcome on a higher level. So in the book of Jeremiah a new covenant is expected in which all instruction from without disappears because there will be an immediate relation between God and man. "And no longer shall each man teach his neighbour and

[2] Goethe, *Faust*, Part I.
[3] Franz Werfel.

each his brother, saying, 'Know the Lord', for they shall all know me, from the least of them to the greatest" (Jer. xxxi.34). In the same way when people are in the closest human relationships possible upon earth it occurs to them that there should be a communion between "I" and "thou" in which we should need no words to understand each other and to act in full mutual comprehension.

This rejection of all religion of the word or religion of the book therefore is based on a right feeling. The fact that God chooses the terrestrial form of verbal communication excludes the immediate relation in which we should be to God if we were not estranged from Him. God's essence and will should be as immediately open to us, as our body is to the three-dimensional space into which we can see immediately. Instead of that we have a relationship to God like the relationship of our three-dimensional space to a totally different space, which within our space remains invisible and inconceivable. We can grasp God's Being only in so far as it is translated from His incomprehensible essence into the language of our own form of existence.

Far greater yet than the judgment that is contained in words as a form of communication, is the unfathomable gift which we receive, in the fact that with a world which He ought to destroy God enters into such close contact as within space is possible only between co-ordinated part-spaces of a comprehensive space. He enters into the same level as ourselves. Let us consider this positive aspect of the *"Deus dixit"*, while for the moment still disregarding the content of God's Word, of which we shall later have to speak in detail, and merely directing our attention to the form of speech. Let us apply what we said above about speech as such to God's speech. Speaking consists in this: that from the great number of sounds which reach my ear, a phonetic figuration distinguishes itself as the sign by which someone else seeks contact with me and addresses himself to my will. The other one who is speaking is by his essence closed to me. But I know that the distinction of this phonetic figuration of sound from surrounding sounds and noises proceeds from him. For it belongs to the essence of the word that I myself cannot speak it. The other must speak the saving word. He must be the speaker.

CHAPTER 18

The Contrast between God's Speech and God's Silent Action

WE ARE NOT open to the biblical message that God has spoken until we have first understood the fundamental difference between the two ways in which a "thou" can approach me: speech and silent action; that is to say the difference between the explaining word and speechless killing, a mute handshake, a silent embrace. We have to regard from this point of view the dividing line which is drawn in the Bible between the one point where God speaks and all other events in the world in which He acts silently. Any speaking presupposes that silence has gone before. The word distinguishes itself only from the dark foil of silence. If there is no silence the speaker cannot make himself understood at all. His words then are drowned in noise. Therefore there is no understanding of the word of God in all those philosophies which do not acknowledge the distinction between these two forms of God's presence, silence and speech, which hold the opinion either that God is equally beyond reach everywhere, or that He can be experienced everywhere in the same way and is always equally near. To Nihilism, to which the Absolute is an inconceivable thought, the thought of a speaking God is also, of course, mythology. "God" is the silent nothing, the yawning emptiness, the insoluble question behind all things. But we are equally unreceptive to the message that God has spoken if, though rejecting the comfortless thought that God is the silent nothing, we think instead that God reveals Himself in the same manner everywhere and at all times, that He speaks to us exactly the same in the awakening of life and in the pain of death as He does in the prophetic words of religious leaders. This view too knows only a revelation of God which is the same everywhere. It does not know the distinction by which the Word stands out brightly from the background of silence.

This identification of action and speech, this mixing up of God's speaking and silence is found not only in mystical pantheism, to which all that happens is a wave in God's ocean, but also in cases where, though believing in a transcendent Creator, we assume that we can draw conclusions as to the meaning and purpose of His creation immediately from the ordinances of nature and the structure of human society. If this were possible, then the order of creation would already be God's open book in which we could read what God wants of us and what we can receive from Him. If God deems it necessary to give us further revelation then this can only repeat what has already been clearly stated in the order of creation, or be no more than a confirmation of the latter. If we have already been instructed concerning all that is important by the book of nature we are no longer capable of an unbiased hearing of what God still adds. For God can never contradict Himself. Of all that religious prophets say we need listen only to that which corresponds with the picture of God's existence and will, that we have drawn from the order of creation as we understand it. We already have a measure in hand to decide what God can have said and what He can certainly not have said. His "commandments" can only be a commentary on the order of creation. Prophetic words and sacred writings, as for example in the Vedantic religion and in Buddhism, can never do more than express in classical form what lives in the heart of every man who goes through the world with open eyes.

The men of the Old Testament, however, adopted an entirely different attitude to the words of God which they received. They were more than any of us under the crushing impression of God's majestic actions in nature and history. In lightning and thunder, in snow and rainstorm, in the neighing of horses and in the crawling of deep-sea monsters the poet of Job (ch. xxxviiff) saw the All-powerful who lives in all things and whom we men cannot resist. All these overpowering impressions of God's omnipotence and majesty had made the question to which we must have an answer if we are not to perish, the question on what terms this Almighty whom we perceive in storm and weather is with us and what He wants of us, even more burning and insoluble to the men of prayer of the Old Testament.

They did not make bold to anticipate the divine answer to this question by rash conclusions from nature and from history in so far as we understand it. They knew that we cannot read the answer in nature. We can only receive it through a Word of God that goes beyond any impressions of nature and from which any such impressions receive their interpretation. If this answer from God which we ourselves simply cannot find, this commandment of the Creator which we men cannot think out, is not granted to us from above, as "a light to my path" (Ps. cxix.105), then we walk in darkness. Surrounded by oriental nature, in the midst of historical events of the greatest magnitude in which empires rose and sank, these men of prayer cried out as from the deepest darkness: "Be not deaf to me, lest, if thou be silent to me, I become like those who go down to the pit" (Ps. xxviii.1). "If thy Law had not been my delight, I should have perished in my affliction" (Ps. cxix.92). Always in the midst of times of tremendous historic events hunger was again roused for a word of God, the hunger which Amos means when he says: "Behold, the days are coming, says the Lord God, when I will send a famine on the land; not a famine of bread, nor a thirst for water, but of hearing the words of the Lord. They shall wander from sea to sea, and from north to east; they shall run to and fro, to seek the word of the Lord" (Amos viii.11-12).

We can find this word of God only if it is to us the bread without which we are to die of starvation, if we are prepared ourselves to desist from following nature and obey God. When Abraham was told to kill his only son, on whom the future of his whole tribe depended, he did not protest that the Creator could not demand such a thing, for according to the order of His own creation parents and children were created for one another. Even the fourth commandment of the Decalogue, which joins parents and children together, and the fifth commandment that protects life, are not derived from the law of nature according to which children exist only through their parents and the instinct of self-preservation has been implanted in every living being. God's commandments apply, not because they confirm ordinances of nature but because they are the words of God who alone is able to disclose the true meaning of nature, words of the Creator which we should have to obey just the same if He were to tell us to hate our father and mother or kill our own son.

From this we see that the message that God has spoken must at once be rejected as folly by all those philosophies to which the biblical distinction between God's action and God's speech is non-existent, that is to say not only pantheism but also any other religion according to which God's essence and will is disclosed always and everywhere, whether He is immediately present within our ego, as Idealism believes, or whether we can deduce Him from the events around us. Hunger for the Word of God is found only among people who have realised that all that is within us and around us cannot solve but can only lay before us the question which can find an answer only if there is a Word "that passes through God's mouth".

At this point therefore two kinds of people separate. On the one hand there are those who do not need the Word in order to receive certitude concerning the ultimate question. They may meanwhile retain a quite conservative standpoint regarding the biblical reports. They may even adhere to the orthodox conviction that the Bible is an inspired Book. Nevertheless the truth of that to which the Apostles bear witness is to them no existential question any more than it is to Idealists or Buddhists. To them the Bible is merely the confirmation or illustration of truths which we should know just the same if it had never been written.

On the other hand there are the people to whom the Word is the food without which they would die of starvation, to whom all that happens within them and around them remains a book of fate with seven seals which no man is able to open unless it is opened by the One whose name is "the Word of God" (Rev. v.1-5). These people may perhaps be far removed from ortho-dox belief in the Bible, indeed they may be subject to serious doubts as to whether perhaps the prophets' belief in their inspir-ation is not due to self-deception and maybe only originates in the burning but unsatisfiable longing of man for a saving word of God. But they know better than those believers in inspiration that to us men there is only this either-or: either we live by every word that passes through the mouth of God, or we have to die of starvation.

All that must now be said about the testimony of the New

Testament can be understood only by the second kind of people. To all others it is folly, an answer to a question which does not even exist. Only if we no longer make any mistake as to the fact that there are only these two possibilities for us shall we not immediately reject as an impossibility the unbelievable message that God Himself has taken in hand the distinction obliterated by all extra-biblical philosophies, the distinction between God's silent action and his speech. Now it is all-important that we learn to see the demarcation line by which a certain content is here distinguished from its surroundings. What does it mean if God is present in our world not merely as One who acts but also as One who speaks? To see this we shall have to start from what speaking actually is, and then transfer this from our human conditions to the relationship with God which is not comparable to any human relation.

We have seen that speech is the form in which a being makes itself known within the space of another person without their condition of being closed to each other ceasing for one moment. The inapproachability of "thou" which gives its character to human speech acquires an absolute character when we are dealing with God speaking. For God's being does not merely remain foreign and inscrutable to us as a human "thou" who is concealed from us. Our relation to God is not merely separation but conflict. For we belong to a world created by God but inhabited by a satanic will which on every point wages war against God to destroy Him.

Consequently, according to John's Gospel, the relationship between God and the world is a war between light and darkness. The light wants to overcome the darkness, but the darkness wants to swallow the light. "The light shines in the darkness, and the darkness apprehended it not (has not overcome it, R.S.V.)" (Jn. 1.5). In the presence of God we realise that the two earthly possibilities open to us when we seek for an answer to the ultimate question, pantheism as well as the deification of a relative quantity, are never anything else but two contrasting forms of idolatry, two directions in which we move to dethrone God. If God approaches us, who by the whole form of our existence are engaged in a movement contrary to Him, by the indirect form of the Word in which He Himself remains hidden, then this is His gracious consideration for us. For we should not be able to bear God's immediate presence. It would kill us. "You cannot see my face; for man shall not see me and live" (Ex. XXXIII.20, 23). "The Lord your God is a devouring fire" (Deut. IV.24; Heb. XII.29). The incarnate Word therefore, which restores a mediated relationship between God and ourselves is according to Melanchthon a cover or shade, an *umbraculum amplectens nos et tegens nostras sordes* (a shade that embraces us and covers our dirtiness).[1]

According to what was said above the essence of speech is that it is the meeting of two spaces co-ordinated in the same comprehensive space, as for example a human ego meets a human "thou" on the same level of this universe. If therefore God who determines all things speaks to us, then He has emptied Himself in so doing. He has assumed the form of a servant and become relative. He has translated His essence into the language of the created state which is contrary to Himself. He has, as Bezzel expresses it, "humbled himself down" to us and has entered into the state of *condescentia*. He has given Himself up into a condition that is contrary to His own essence. We can assume that this surrender must lead to a severe clash.

Two spaces of the same grade, as we saw, can intersect only within a comprehending space which embraces both, that is to say: lines only within a plane, planes only within three-dimensional space, "I" and "thou" only in a comprehending medium which we have called world-space. If therefore God empties Himself and encounters us as a speaking "Thou" on our own level, then we must assume the existence of a comprehending medium within which the encounter takes place and which makes the encounter possible. This medium in virtue of which the intersection of the divine and the creaturely sphere is effected the Bible calls the Holy Ghost. He is the ground which makes possible the encounter mediated by the Word. Therefore it is through Him alone that the place within the created world where God speaks is distinguished from the remaining content of the world. It is through Him that the dividing line comes into being, the understanding of which is of the utmost importance, the line that distinguishes between God's silence and God's speaking. It is through Him that a

[1] Hans Engelland, *Melanchthon*, Munich 1931, pp. 499, 318.

place in the temporal world receives the accent of Eternity.

The distinction which comes into being here can be regarded only from two sides, from God's side and from ours. For if God speaks it is He who separates a content of this world from its surroundings and places it in the light of Eternity. And yet at the same time the separation always takes place within the space of our existence. For speech comes into being only if there is a listener to receive it. A word that fades away without being heard is not a word at all but an empty sound. For according to its true nature a word is not an object but an act in which speaking and hearing takes place. Consequently when God speaks, those to whom His word is addressed must perceive the dividing line that separates the content through which He speaks from all others.

According to the Scriptures therefore the Spirit of God, the Ground which makes the encounter between God and the creature possible, always has two simultaneous functions, which are however two sides of one and the same divine act. On the one hand the Spirit of God elects from God's side the created organ through which God speaks. This is the divine "election" which as an all-prevailing category determines the whole of biblical thought. Men through whom God speaks are conscious that contrary to any desires and inclinations of their own they have by an inescapable destiny been set apart from birth to say something in God's name. The Spirit of God has earmarked them, as the forester marks with an axe the tree to be felled.

The second function of the Spirit, which is merely the other side of the same divine act, consists in the fact that the demarcation line that comes into being by God's sovereign election is made visible to those with whom God desires to enter into communication. For the content which is set apart here is found within the universe which comprehends us, exactly like any other content which we can perceive. It is within the time-spatial causal connexion of earthly experience. No one can perceive the eternal accent on this one place in time "but in the Holy Spirit". He whose eyes the Spirit does not open, whose "eyes are holden", cannot see anything at this place that does not fit in the framework of the whole. To him the phenomenon is relative to all other events.

The demarcation line therefore that comes into being is drawn in a manner which is contrary to the entire nature of time. Consequently it has nothing to do with any immanent distinction which would be visible to everybody. It is neither a distinction of power nor of aesthetics. It does not consist in the contrast between strength and weakness, between the heroic and the ordinary, between personalities of genius and insignificant people. Divine election works sovereignly, regardless of all these deep terrestrial norms and distinctions of magnitude. The line which God draws here, through which the eternal light falls on one spot in contrast to the whole shadowed world of transience, is therefore visible to us only if God Himself opens our eyes. But then it shines so clearly that all other distinctions become irrelevant as compared with it.

If the Spirit opens our eyes so that we see a content of the world illuminated from above by the light of eternity as by a search-light, then we experience very really that a comprehending sphere surrounds us as the medium in which the encounter between God and ourselves takes place, as a space of higher order that bears and embraces us. While hearing the Word I am called back to my *origin*, to the state in which I should always have been and in which I would be if estrangement from God had not disturbed my existence. I should then have remained in God as in a space in which one is safe and from which one cannot fall away. While hearing the Word I am called back to this being in God as the lost paradise in which I receive a right again to live.

We therefore see that although we have said nothing so far about the content which, to him whose eyes have been opened, distinguishes itself from its surroundings as God's Word, although we have moved in purely formal definitions without blood and life, yet even the purely formal statement that God has spoken at all already leads us to the Trinitarian formula. The way and manner in which God's eternal being is translated into the language of time necessarily implies a threefold content in inseparable unity: (1) the unfathomable Being of God Himself; (2) that part-content of the world which God, in emptying Himself, sets apart within the world as His Word; (3) the comprehending ground which makes the encounter possible, the Spirit, the medium, the space in which the encounter takes place. In this Word and Spirit belong insepar-ably together.

Enthusiasts of all times have sought to pass by the instrument of the Word which creates a mediated relationship between God and us and to break through to an immediate relationship to God. This is a titanic effort to break down the barrier made by the estrangement of our existence from God, i.e. to force the gate of paradise lost before which stands the cherub with the drawn sword. But there is for us no fellowship with God inde-pendent of and apart from the Word embodied in Christ through which He speaks to us. The medium of the Spirit which restores communion between God and us can come into force only if a content of this world is delineated as the Word through which God enters into communion with us. As the Word cannot become visible without the Spirit, so the Spirit cannot restore communion between the two worlds without the Word.

CHAPTER 19

God Has Spoken by the Son

So far we have described the event, which according to the witness of the New Testament is more important than all other historical events put together, in general outline as the place where God has come forth from His silent action and has spoken. We shall now have to draw the circle a little narrower and look at the content itself, which is of this unique importance.

In considering the general form of communication through words we have already seen that the demarcation line separating the word from its environment can be drawn and made visible only by the Speaker himself. Only if the Spirit opens my ear can I hear, among all the other voices around me, the silver voice of the Shepherd who calls me back to where my origin is. Without the work of the Spirit I lack the ability to distinguish and the voice of the Shepherd is drowned in the ocean of other sounds. If the Spirit alone is able to make visible the place where God speaks then not only is every effort on my part to find this place with the aid of some heuristic principle futile, but the very fact that I undertake it shows that I have misunderstood my situation in relation to God. As soon as I attempt to use any general principle belonging to the content of my own mind as a starting point from which to make deductions as to where and how God has spoken, then I have forgotten that I am in an ungodly condition in which I cannot by myself know anything at all of God's decisions, and that therefore I cannot learn what He wants unless He Himself speaks to me. It belongs to the essence of the word, that the speaker alone is active and giving, while the hearer is merely the passive and receptive vessel.

Therefore it is only in the narrative style of the apostles, as a fact, without any explanation or reason, that we can state that God has spoken in the historical appearance of a man who is placed in the midst of the billions of people who have moved on this earth. God has taken up contact with us in a living "Thou" which stands in the midst of all the other "thous" but by an invisible dividing line has been set apart from all the others as the One who has authority.

This event could not be foreseen. It is not as if God could only make Himself understood by us through a living man, and not, for example, by means of a dead code of law or in some other way. It is not our task to make statements on God's possibilities of coming to terms with us. Only after the event, since God has confronted us with the *fait accompli*, are we in a position to reflect on this.

These reflexions cannot lead us to understand the ultimate why of this fact. We can only retrace the accomplished fact in reflexion and make clear its import. As little as we can deduce from a general principle the fact that God had to speak to us through a human personality, so little can we deduce from any general presupposition through which human being God would speak, on which historical figure the emphasis would fall. If we want to hear the answer which God has given to the question on which our whole destiny depends, then it is all-important for us to become complete hearers in respect of this answer and not to interrupt the Speaker in any way. Only in this attitude can we hear what the Spirit says when He comes down and sets this one Man apart from all other men as an organ of God's self-revelation, with these words: "This is my beloved Son, with whom I am well pleased; listen to him!" (Mt. XVII.8).

Natural man already takes offence at God's speaking as such because the fact of being spoken to from without reminds him in a humbling way of his ungodly condition. But after God has spoken the defensive attitude of man towards the Word of God enters into a second stage. If a foreign body, e.g. a shell splinter, has penetrated into an organism and the latter is unable to eject it, then it tries to render it harmless by enveloping it and so making it part of itself. In the same way, as we cannot undo the divine decision which has elected a certain person as its organ, we attempt at least to make it harmless by deducing it as a necessity from the presuppositions of our own reflexion. In this way we are freed of the unpleasant feeling that we are condemned to passivity as regards the ultimate question. We have got hold of the divine solution ourselves and can abandon ourselves to the proud conviction that, at least by our reflexion, we ourselves have produced it.

This has been achieved most brilliantly by Hegel in his lectures on the philosophy of religion. He first attempted to demonstrate that the Absolute was bound to become incarnate not in a plurality but only in an individual who through death attained to the resurrection. "To the true consciousness of the spirit the finiteness of man has been killed in the death of Christ on the cross."[1] "The immediateness of the existing individuality is dissolved, and this is done through death; but the death of Christ is the death of this death, the negation of the negation."[2]

Speculative construction entered even more deeply into the details of the event. The death of Jesus must be "the extreme point of finiteness". To this end it is not sufficient that it is merely a death as such. "Apart from being a natural death it is also the death of a criminal, the most dishonourable death upon the cross."[3] This too is necessary according to thought. For the "objective" being of man, his conceptual existence, is his position in the estimation of others, i.e. his honour. If therefore the entire finiteness of man is to be negatived in order to be saved through the negation, then natural death is not enough. It must be a death which also destroys the estimation in other people's eyes, that is to say "the death of a criminal, the most dishonourable death on the cross . . . the cross corresponds with our gallows".[4]

This whole demonstration, the details of which are of no consequence to us in this connexion, is a typical example of how man parries with dexterous dialectical evasion the crushing blow which God's incomprehensible solution deals to his self-consciousness. It has pleased God to speak to us through One who was dishonourably slain, the course of whose life Celsus sums up in the significant words: "A wretched death ended a despicable life." But man does not allow this to disconcert him. He is at once master of the situation again. He says: I could have predicted this result. It follows from the dialectics

---

[1] Hegel, *Werke*, ed. G. Lasson, Leipzig 1920-44, VOL. XIV, p. 175.
[2] *Op. cit.*, p. 167.   [3] *Op. cit.*, p. 161.   [4] Ibid.

present in the essence of the spirit. "Spirit is spirit only as this negation of the negation which the negation thus contains within itself." "Therefore, what this life of Christ represents, and that to the empirical, general and immediate consciousness, is this process of the nature of the spirit, God in human form. This process in its development is the progress of the divine Idea to the ultimate dissension, to the contrary of the pain of death, which itself is the absolute reversal, the highest love, which in itself is the negation of the negation, the absolute reconciliation, the elimination of the opposition of man to God and the end, present as a dissolution in glory, the glorious assumption of the human into the Idea of the Divine. The first, God in human form, he really is in this process, which shows the separation of the divine Idea and its reunion, its completion as truth. This is the whole of history."[5]

If we embark on such an attempt to deduce *ex post facto* God's decision from the dialectic relation between time and Eternity as we understand it, then we show that we have entirely misjudged our position in relation to God. We have abandoned the only attitude in which we can hear what God wishes to say. Then we still do not know that listening means to desist from any construction of our own. Through these constructions of our mind, which bypass our organ of vision for reality, we can only receive an imaginary Christ. We remain within the circle of our own possibilities and either imagine God's organ of revelation as an ideal picture of human greatness and heroism or as the same ideal picture with a negative sign, that is to say as the "extreme of finiteness", as the nadir of human poverty, humility, disgrace and dishonour.

This second, negative picture does not even hold good in every respect of the real Jesus of Nazareth. According to the historical records one will have to say: "The family to which Jesus belonged must have been well-to-do. Jesus' cousins as farmers in Nazareth cultivated their own land: in view of the infrequency of change of property in those days this was probably inherited from their grandfather. Moreover Joseph had his occupation as a τέκτων, which is not correctly translated by 'carpenter' but rather indicates a builder, who builds houses, castles, temples, ships, etc. . . . In view of the timber trade in

[5] Hegel, *Werke*, ed. G. Lasson, Leipzig 1920-44, VOL. XIV, p. 163f.

Palestine the buying and the working of wood was certainly the most important aspect of the building business. In itself it needed a man of means because the purchase and transport of a stock of timber was expensive. In his workshop Joseph also produced ploughs, weapons, yokes and other agricultural implements so that the whole must have been a considerable business, in which Jesus worked as a youth and as a man."[6] Anything that we can deduce from the idea of Absoluteness and relativity, infinity and finiteness, and from the relation between them is therefore valueless in respect of the reality of Jesus.

It is a further misunderstanding of our situation if we think that out of the many religious leaders who offer themselves to us we can choose on the basis of an inner feeling the one who meets our real need. For if in the question which is here at issue there is to be any sense at all in choosing a leader, then we should need an instinct that enables us to find among the many religious prophets who offer themselves the one who shows the right direction in the same way as an animal in a meadow avoids with sure instinct the poisonous plants which are dangerous to it and finds the plants which serve to feed it. To make a choice, whether it is a question of choosing a friend or electing a political leader, we must first have a scale of values, a certain preference or a guiding point of view which makes it possible for us to prefer one among the possible personalities.

If we had such a norm by which we could decide who is the true leader for the solution of the ultimate question, then we should be capable of guiding ourselves. Then we should no longer need God's self-revelation. Autonomous choice of a leader is merely another form of self-guidance. We should then have access to the solution of the question concerning Eternity simply in virtue of our natural equipment. Then God would have supplied us with the sure instinct on the path of life, enabling us to find our bearings, by the mere fact of creation. God then need not have gone beyond His silently creative activity and started to speak. But we need Christ as the Word of God incarnate for the very reason that we are not capable of choosing a leader.

[6] F. Frh. von Edelsheim, *Das Evangelium nach Markos*, Leipzig 1931.

M

Therefore it is a misunderstanding of the meaning of Jesus if we give Him a place in a pantheon of religious leaders of mankind together with Buddha, Confucius, Lao-tze, Plato, etc., and think that we could have their programme on approval and then choose whichever appeals to us. Jesus certainly does not desire a place in a pantheon of heroes of the spirit. His mission begins only at the point where all these leaders have failed and were bound to fail. The meaning of His task becomes manifest only after we have realised that all mankind's attempts to solve the question of meaning by its own strength under the guidance of these great minds cannot deliver us from uncertainty. The programmes of the great leaders, Buddha's denial of the desire to live, Nietzsche's dynamic intoxication with life, and again Confucius's matter-of-fact disciplined order, show by their very mutual contradictions that we men can only make groping attempts to find the way out of the dark prison in which we are locked up. The lack of unanimity among the leaders confirms the judgment which the prologue of the Gospel according to John passes on the universal condition of mankind, when it speaks of the darkness into which the light penetrates only when God begins to speak (Jn. 1.4).

CHAPTER 20

The Testimony of God's Revelation in Christ

WHAT HAS BEEN discussed so far has first of all made us realise the negative fact that by nature we have at our disposal no criteria by which to recognise whether and where and how God has spoken to us. When God speaks to us, then He Himself has to open our eyes for us to see the place where He discloses Himself to us. "Through God alone can God be known."[1] We can speak of this speech of God's only as men whose eyes He has opened so that they see this place. In this sense we testify together with the apostles first of all to the fundamental fact: God has spoken to us not through an "it" but through a "Thou". At the same time this indicates the only way in which we can testify to God's Word.

If the organ through which God speaks to us were an "it", that is to say something that we have before us objectively, whether it be a natural phenomenon or a table of laws or a code of law or a general principle, then it would be the task of the messenger to establish an "I-it" relationship between us and this "it", i.e. to make its content visible with photographic accuracy in its objective reality, as in a darkened archaeological lecture room one reproduces a lantern slide of an ancient temple ruin in such clear light that every column head and every ornament meets the eye of the viewer with plastic clarity.

The task of the witness is completely different if God does not speak through an "it" but through a "Thou". As shown in Vol. I[2] the very manner in which a "Thou" meets us is something different from the way in which an object confronts us. The contrast between the two, however, can be understood only from the point of view of a dynamic philosophy. A dynamic philosophy teaches us that all that is is not constant by itself. On the contrary at every moment it is born anew from

---

[1] Emil Brunner, *Der Mittler*, Tübingen 1927, p. 3; Engl. trans. *The Mediator*, by Olive Wyon, London 1934, p. 21.   [2] *God Transcendent* (pp. 103-173).

nothing. What remains stays alive only because there is a power which, in spite of all the powers endeavouring to remove it, ordains it anew from moment to moment. In this process of continued creation and transition in which every moment a decision is made on its future form, the "it" and the "thou" take opposite parts. "It" is the world in the state of being finished. Only in this stage can one look upon it as a spectator. "Thou" on the contrary encounters me in the battle for the future form of the world, according to circumstances either as an opponent or as an ally or in whatever other role may be possible on the battlefield for a new world. What "thou" means therefore cannot be expressed in an objective form at all. Only the negative fact is clear: "Thou" has a meaning which cannot be determined objectively but can be perceived only by the warrior. Words spoken by someone else, in so far as they have already been spoken by the time I hear them, have indeed the "it" character of an objectively given condition. But I hear them as the words of a "thou" only if I do not receive them merely as objectively given, and take notice of them, e.g. like special cases of grammatical rules or etymological laws, or receive them as descriptions of a state of affairs which has to be explained to me, according to the Greek-Hellenistic meaning of the word *Logos*.[3] I hear them as the words of a "thou" only if I feel the fiery breath of the battle, that is to say if they are to me the expression of a will which takes part in the battle for the shaping of the world and which addresses me, not as a spectator but in the way in which one appeals to a man who has been called to fight the same battle. If I hear these words as the words of a "thou", then I know that the being who is speaking here is more than those words. However important certain words or actions may be for an understanding of the speaker, yet they are merely detached, lightning-like discharges of a power behind those words. The speaker himself is behind those deposits of his will as the living source from which many more words and actions come forth.

If this is the essence of "thou" as contrasted with "it" and if it has pleased God to speak to us through a "thou", then we cannot witness to Him who is God's Word incarnate by de-

---

[3] Rudolf Bultmann, *Glauben und Verstehen*, 2nd edn., Tübingen 1954, VOL. I, pp. 274ff.

scribing His objective appearance in the manner of an historian; then we should have treated Him as if he were merely an "it". Nor can the heedfulness[4] in which we stand before a "thou" through whom God speaks to us, be expressed in an enthusiastic description, in the manner of a poet describing his hero. If as beings co-operating responsibly in the shaping of the world we take a "thou" seriously as a "thou", then, having regard to all that has already been said concerning the "I-thou" relationship, this is possible only in one way. We must hear his words as commandments which call us to a definite attitude in the present situation.

The word commandment is taken in its broadest sense here. We are dealing with a commandment not only if the words have the actual form of a command – beginning "Thou shalt" – which tells me either actively to advance to the attack or passively to remain under cover. A word of judgment, condemning past action, if I take the judge seriously as a "thou", is heard as a commandment to desist in future from the indictable action and as far as possible to make amends. A promise too, which prophesies a glorious future, I hear, if I take the prophet seriously as a "thou", as the commandment: "Do not throw away your confidence which has a great reward!" (Heb. x.35).

In all these cases therefore the "I-thou" relationship has been really established only if I hear in his word the commandment that applies to my present situation. I cannot meet a commandment by neutral reflexion. Neutrality, even if dressed in the form of an enthusiastic report in the press or of subtle psychological observation, is disobedience if applied to a commandment. That is why all real leaders have had a definite dislike of the incense of admiration and enthusiastic ovations. They sensed that here was a particularly dangerous form of escaping from the only thing that mattered, the obedience of the deed. "Why do you call me 'Lord, Lord', and not do what I tell you?" (Lk. vi.46).

Therefore, as soon as I hear the words of a "thou" as commandments, there are only two possibilities in relation to him; obedience or rebellion. From this it follows that if God comes to us in the form of a human person of whom He says: "This

---

[4] *Hörigkeit* means both the attitude of listening and the state of serfdom. Tr.

is my beloved Son, listen to him!", then we can witness to this
fact in one way only. We must ourselves become obedient to
Him, that is to say assume the attitude of unqualified surrender,
and in and from this attitude emphatically point to the One
under whose guidance alone we are on the way to God, in the
same way as the voice at His baptism indicated to Him, and
as the forerunner John pointed to Him with the words: "Behold,
the Lamb of God, who takes away the sin of the world" (Jn.
1.29). All narratives and descriptions are merely means to
this end.

Strictly speaking our testimony cannot go beyond this point-
ing, if the One to whom we point really is the One who has the
authority to guide every man to the end of his destiny. For if
He really is the Lord of all men, then His guidance starts the
moment a man to whom He has been pointed out has come
into contact with Him and is prepared to listen to Him, in
other words as soon as the "thou" relationship has really come
into force. For a "thou" relationship is in the first place not a
relationship between a Leader and the masses but between
"I" and "thou", that is a relationship between two persons.
Everyone therefore who is called to follow Christ must be personally bound to the Leader by an individual pledge. Only
through the fact that everyone who is called has a personal
relationship to Him, which is known only to him, does there
come into being the unique formation of the "Body of Christ"
of which the New Testament speaks. For every member of
the Body has an immediate relationship to the Soul that
governs the Body and which is present at every point. That is
how they all become members in relation to one another
(1 Cor. XII). In this way one cannot interfere with the life of
another by communicating one's own thoughts to him but
only by becoming an agent of the Leader and delivering the
Leader's order or promise to him. But the order or the promise
which someone else delivers to me in the name of the Leader
has authority only if at the same time as I hear the word which
a brother communicates to me, I can make immediate contact
with the Leader Himself so that I hear the word of the disciple
immediately as the Word of the Master.

The testimony to Christ, as voiced within the Church, even
if it does consist of narratives of Jesus' words and deeds, ulti-

mately does not have the intention to depict the historical figure of Jesus. It always wants to bring the hearer into personal contact with Him so that His guidance can come into force. According to the Gospels Jesus Himself was not in the first place concerned with giving those who listened to Him a doctrine or a philosophy. On the contrary He wishes to bring them into a personal relationship to Himself, a relationship which consists in their listening to Him as the Leader accredited by God.

This contact with Him, which is the real issue, consists in this, that He becomes to them the One for whose sake they do and suffer whatever they do and suffer, whose command does not need a higher authority because it is given in the name of the Absolute. "Blessed are you when men revile you and persecute you and utter all kinds of evil against you falsely on my account. Rejoice and be glad, for your reward is great in heaven" (Mt. v.11-12). "And whoever loses his life for my sake and the gospel's will save it" (Mk. viii.35). "For whoever is ashamed of me and of my words in this adulterous and sinful generation, of him will the Son of man also be ashamed when he comes in the glory of his Father with the holy angels" (Mk. viii.38). During the meal that has been handed down to us as the miraculous feeding of the multitude He shares out food to every one by His own hand. This is a liturgical meal in view of the Messianic meal. . . . The only thing therefore Jesus is concerned about is that everyone receives from His own hand some of the food dedicated to Him and so enters into eating fellowship with Him.[5] He who receives a child in His name receives Him. On the day of judgment men will be declared by the Son of Man to be just and to be participants in the Kingdom "forasmuch as they have given Him food when He was hungry, have given Him to drink when He was thirsty, have given Him shelter when He was a stranger, have given Him clothes when He was naked, have visited Him when He was ill, have come to see Him when He was in prison. To their astonished question when they have done such a thing to him, they receive the answer that they have done it to one of

[5] Albert Schweitzer, *Die Mystik des Apostels Paulus*, Tübingen 1930, p. 108; Engl. trans. *The Mysticism of Paul the Apostle*, by W. Montgomery, London 1931, p. 107.

the least of His brothers and therein have done it to Him."[6]

The tragic outcome, in human terms, of the life of Jesus is caused by the very fact that He has to act in such a way that men can always follow Him only for His own sake, because of the divine authority within Him, and not for any purely human reason. Therefore He has continually to wage war on two fronts, against His enemies and against those who honour Him on false grounds. He has to repel and to disappoint all those who want to enthuse about Him because He fulfils for them some human desire. The people applaud Him because of His miracles and follow Him in large crowds. It would have been an easy matter for Him to get the masses completely on His side and to be acclaimed as the universally revered leader of the people and a political Messiah. He could have been popular at once if He had only made a minor compromise in this respect. But He says: "An evil and adulterous generation seeks for a sign, but no sign shall be given to it" (Mt. xvi.4). When after the miraculous feeding of the multitude they want to get hold of Him, to make Him king, then, according to John's Gospel, He withdraws to the mountain alone, and when He is among the people again later He says: "Truly, truly, I say to you, you seek me, not because you saw signs but because you ate your fill of the loaves. Do not labour for the food which perishes, but for the food which endures to eternal life, which the Son of man will give to you" (Jn. vi.26-7).

From a political point of view therefore Jesus acts extremely unwisely. He lets all chances slip by without making use of them. He misses all opportunities of gaining power. He immediately seeks to destroy any nimbus that forms around Him. He even forbids the promulgation of His miracles of healing. Only once does He accept homage, and this consists in His being anointed for His burial. Even within the circle of the disciples He does not allow any fanatical adoration to arise.

As a result of this the history of His activity develops in a direction contrary to that which we observe in the career of other historical personalities. Others too have begun with a small band of followers. But then the number of adherents has

[6] Albert Schweitzer, *Die Mystik des Apostels Paulus*, Tübingen 1930, p. 109; Engl. trans. *The Mysticism of Paul the Apostle*, by W. Montgomery, London 1931, p. 108.

continually increased until they have filled the world with their fame. This is the development which Goethe illustrates in *Mahomets Gesang*; the mountain spring reaches the plain as a river and ultimately increases to a mighty stream that discharges itself into the ocean. But the course of Jesus' life goes in the opposite direction. In the beginning it is a popular movement. Then, disappointed and irritated, more and more followers turn their backs on Him, and it is said: "After this many of his disciples drew back" (Jn. vi.66). "This is the mystery of suffering; this 'Will you also go away?' sounds so pained: shall I then, who came to save all men – will it come to this that there is no man whose salvation I shall be? To stand there with open arms, and all men run away scandalised."[7] Before the night of the Passion He has to tell the nearest circle of his disciples: "You will all fall away because of me this night" (Mt. xxvi.31).

This whole course of the life of Jesus is understandable only because He has an aim that is contrary to that of any other historical personality. What He desired was not power and influence, He did not want to create a party machinery, or establish an order or start a philosophical school. His task, which during the temptation after His baptism had once and for all become clear to Him, was to live in such a way that there would be only two possibilities left in connexion with Him. Either we are scandalised and turn away from Him in disappointment because He does not allow Himself to be used for our purposes. Or even at the lowest point of His weakness we love Him for His own sake and carry His cross behind Him.

If the whole world had applauded Him because He had made a concession, however small, to its desires for bread and power, then in the eyes of Eternity this would have been only a defeat. But when, lonely and misunderstood by all, He dies, afterwards to be loved by a few Galilean fishermen and publicans, then to the world this is a wretched failure as Celsus says: "a despicable life that ends in a wretched death" but to God a glorious victory.

Even if Jesus had not said so repeatedly, His whole fate in life would show that His aim was not to gain followers for a moral teaching or for a philosophy, but to get people, even

[7] Cf. S. Kierkegaard, *Training in Christianity*, trans. W. Lowrie, London 1941, p. 107.

though only an exceedingly small number, so far that for His sake they leave everything and follow Him, accepting unconditionally whatever He commands.

CHAPTER 21

Our Contemporariness with Christ

IF ACCORDING to the report of the Gospels Jesus called the people of those days to be His personal followers, then for us, who are separated from the days of Christ by nearly 2,000 years, the question arises: is it not the case that it is only possible for those who lived at the same time as Jesus to be His personal followers, as He wished? To be His personal follower always presupposes a "thou" relationship. Is not this out of the question for those who live afterwards, who have not "eaten and drunk together with Him"? The whole present importance of Jesus depends on this.

Bultmann, to whom in other respects we owe valuable knowledge for an understanding of the New Testament faith in Christ, clearly emphasises his disagreement with Emanuel Hirsch and others when he says: "In what sense then can He be 'personally quite near to us so that it comes to a live discourse?' It is obvious that He cannot be a 'thou' in the same sense as a man to whom we are linked in the present."[1] "Indeed as regards those attempts 'to dive into the heart of the Crucified' one must frankly say: I cannot see what advantage the historical Jesus who meets his death in obedient love has in the least over all those who, e.g. in the World War met their death in obedient love, and whose course not only means more to us because it is more observable but especially because we were linked to them as a living 'thou'. To want to have such experiences with a person of the past, seems to me artificial and leads to sentimentality."[2]

But then according to Bultmann the "thou"-relation to Jesus, which he regards as impossible, must not be replaced by a representation of a picture of the historical Jesus, the imaginative preoccupation with the picture of the Crucified, the astonishing impression of His historical personality, as was

[1] *Glauben und Verstehen*, VOL. I, p. 97.   [2] *Op. cit.*, p. 96.

habitual in the outdated theology of the historical Jesus. For Bultmann sees correctly that this would establish merely an "it"-relationship to Jesus. We should then be preoccupied merely with "Christ according to the flesh", inasmuch as He belongs to the "sphere of what is empirically present".[3] That would not be the obedience which we owe Him as the Word of God.

But if in relation to Christ not only is the "thou"-relation impossible but the "it"-relationship is also excluded, then our obedience of faith cannot have Him as its content any longer. It can only be surrender to what God has done in Christ. The saving act of God consists in this: that He "is God's Word, that in the preaching of this Word the hour of decision has come, that he who hears Him hears the Father, he who sees Him sees the Father, he who honours Him honours the Father".[4]

But then, as Bultmann himself explains in his essay on the concept of the Word of God in the New Testament,[5] it belongs to the very essence of the Word in the New Testament sense that it does not explain a state of affairs to me but is a commandment. But a commandment must always have a concrete content. It must call me to a definite behaviour in my present situation. If therefore Jesus is the incarnate Word of God to which in my present situation I can listen in such a way that I hear the Father, then it is not sufficient if His memory makes me realise in general the seriousness of my responsibility before God. If need be the thought of death or the memory of great examples like Socrates or Confucius would also be sufficient to strengthen my sense of responsibility. If the inconceivable does happen that God in Christ really gives me His Word, which He speaks right into my present situation, then this Word must really be what between man and man we mean by a word, viz. a call to a definite action. Obedience, and in case of refusal disobedience and judgment, is possible only in relation to such a call. "And that servant who knew his master's will . . . shall receive a severe beating" (Lk. xii.47).

This leads us to the inevitable conclusion: Jesus can be the Word of God incarnate only if we men of the present who have

---

[3] *Glauben und Verstehen*, vol. I, p. 258.   [4] *Op. cit.*, p. 267.
[5] "Der Begriff des Wortes Gottes im neuen Testament" in *Glauben und Verstehen*, vol. I, pp. 268-93.

not lived on earth with Him can also have a "thou"-relation to Him. This may seem incomprehensible to us and contradict any conceptions we may have of the relationship possible between men who are not contemporaries. But we should make no mistake as to this: either it is actually possible for us to enter into a relationship of being contemporary with Christ, like the Early Church, and therefore to be called, guided and commanded by Him; or that which Christians of all centuries have said about their relationship to Christ has been self-deception, autosuggestion, fanciful communion with someone dead, sentimental preoccupation with a product of the imagination. Then our position in relation to God has not become essentially different from what it was before the coming of Christ. Now as before we are without real guidance. There can be no doubt that the whole message of the New Testament is based on the belief that the *Pneuma*, the power of God which in Christ has restored the connexion between God and us, continues after His death to maintain live communication between Him and the Church. According to the farewell discourse in John's Gospel the *Pneuma* after the death of Jesus takes His place as the leading organ. This *Pneuma* reminds the disciples of all that Jesus has said and leads them into all truth, even in questions which Jesus has never mentioned to His disciples. "I have yet many things to say to you, but you cannot bear them now. When the Spirit of truth comes, he will guide you into all the truth; for he will not speak on his own authority, but whatever he hears he will speak, and he will declare to you the things that are to come. He will glorify me, for he will take what is mine and declare it to you. All that the Father has is mine; therefore I said that he will take what is mine and declare it to you" (Jn. XVI.12-15).

Paul too, in cases where there is no historical word of Jesus available for the guidance of the Church – as in the question of marriage – appeals to the guidance of the Spirit which empowers him to give very concrete instructions in the name of Christ (I Cor. VII.25, 40). Indeed, according to II Cor. XII.8-9, he has a confidential conversation with the *Kyrios* about the disease which hinders him in his work, and receives as a commandment for this time the very definite instruction: "My grace is sufficient for you, for my power is made perfect in weakness."

In the Apocalypse the seven churches receive open letters which all introduce themselves as the words of the invisibly present Christ, who speaks right into the particular historical situation of the Church, and which end with the words: "He who has an ear, let him hear what the Spirit says to the churches" (Rev. ii-iii).

The Early Church therefore lived by the belief that through the Spirit God has once and for all authorised Christ to form the living contact between God and us. In other words, since the coming of Christ there has been a decisive change in the history of the relation between God and the world. For all of us who live after this turning-point the Spirit has made this one Person so to speak the focal point where all rays come together. Henceforth He is the permanent medium of the "thou"-relation between God and mankind. Although the few who lived with him as eye- and ear-witnesses have a relative advantage, they have no absolute advantage over all those born later. They are merely the first-fruits of a growing Church, in which all in the same way become the members of His spiritual Body, in which there is a lasting union between Christ and every individual.

We cannot set aside this belief on which the Early Church was based as a myth which was merely the contemporary guise for her impression of this unique personality. On the contrary the whole early Christian message stands or falls on this belief. The relationship between God and mankind has changed fundamentally by the appearance of Jesus only if this is founded on truth. A door has been opened that cannot be closed any more. Admittedly there were words of God again and again before that time. "In many and various ways God spoke of old to our fathers by the prophets . . ." (Heb. 1.1). But these prophetic bearers of the Word were always commissioned with God's words only for a certain historical situation. The Word of God "came to them", as it is said again and again in the Old Testament, afterwards to leave them again. The Word of God therefore could be abstracted from the human vessel that had been called to its proclamation. It had an objective existence of its own, independent of its bearer. But now a fundamental change took place. A person was elected to be the personified Word of God. He was not merely the bearer of the

Word of God who had to pass it on. He was the Word of God itself. Christ was the One of whom it could be said: "The name by which he is called is The Word of God" (Rev. XIX.13).

Thereby a new situation came into being. We can illustrate this most clearly by the parable which according to John's Gospel (IV.13-14) Jesus Himself uses to express that new thing that we have been given by His coming. Beforehand God's speaking was like occasional showers. The water that they produced was gathered in cisterns and kept for some time until it was used or evaporated. But now a live well was substituted for the cisterns in which one had struggled hard to save the remnants of previous showers – a Person from whom the Word of God wells up as from inexhaustible depths. If we have made contact with this living source, then we need no longer be thirsty. God is no longer silent to us. "The times of ignorance" (Acts XVII.30) are past. The "*Abba*, Father", the *original* sound of the soul which had been choked through estrangement from God, becomes audible again (Rom. VIII.15). Within the spiritual Church, this personality of Christ enlarged into a Body, we are no longer dependent on our own decision. There is guidance in which we can trust.

There is therefore an authority to which we can turn, a place where we can go to receive God's Word for our situation. Then there is a clear distinction between the two times distinguished in Heb. 1: the time which is now past, in which God spoke to the fathers by the prophets in many and various ways and places, and the time in which we are now, of which it is said: "(God has) in these last days spoken to us by a Son ... (who), upholding the universe by his word of power . . . sat down at the right hand of the Majesty on high" (Heb. 1.3). This is in no way a depreciation of the manner in which God spoke to the fathers during the period that is now past. At the time it was the highest that was at all possible. It retains its full validity for that time. But we cannot turn back the wheel of time. Even if as yet we have by no means realised the fact, it is our destiny to have been born after the end of that first period, that is to say as children of the final period, the time of Christ. That is why we can no longer immediately apply to ourselves what held good in respect of the fathers. For it belongs to the essence of the word that it applies only to those to whom it is addressed. Under certain circumstances a word which to the fathers was God's Word can no longer be the same to us because God speaks to us in a new language.

The whole message of the New Testament becomes understandable only if it is no fanatical presumption but truth that the New Testament Church of Christ had the living Word of God in its midst as a Person. If she had only had a prophet, i.e. a temporary bearer of the Word whose part was finished when he died, then all her activity should have been concentrated on collecting, preserving and repeating as many of the precious words of the Master as possible, as in the East one preserves as much as possible of the fallen rain-water in cisterns. Instead of this, not only in the Gospel according to Mark but also in the writings of Paul – though he does know the words of the Lord handed down by tradition – the sayings of Jesus remain remarkably in the background. The author of the Gospel according to John also seems to know much about the words and signs of Jesus which, lest he become too loquacious, he does not mention at all. "Now Jesus did many other signs in the presence of the disciples, which are not written in this book" (Jn. xx.30). "But there are also many other things which Jesus did; were every one of them to be written, I suppose that the world itself could not contain the books that would be written" (Jn. xxi.25).

This carelessness about passing on and repeating the words and deeds of the Unique One can be explained only because the messengers were convinced that they were not speaking of a dead but of a living person. If we are speaking about the words and deeds of a person who is still alive and acting, then our speaking can only be intended to introduce him to our hearers. We give them a few classical examples which are particularly characteristic, in order to make them go to himself and listen to himself. We give them a draught from the source of salvation to give them the courage to go to the source themselves. Accordingly it is said at the end of John's Gospel: These signs – which are merely a limited selection from the great number of Christ's works – "are written that you may believe that Jesus is the Christ, the Son of God, and that believing you may have life in his name" (Jn. xx.31).

If the reader is guided to a position of obedience of faith in relation to Christ, then the aim of the report is reached. He finds himself at the Source. Christ can then continue the conversation with them and He will do all that is further required that they may have life. Even in the very form of narrative and report therefore, the testimony of the apostles to Christ is founded on an unlimited confidence in the superior reality of the Spirit, who, since He rests in Christ, is able to bring everyone who is prepared for this into real contact with Christ and who opens the ears for that which the Spirit says to the Church.

The witnesses were unshakeably convinced that men who are prepared to allow themselves to be guided by Christ, do in fact come under the real guidance of the living Lord. For this guidance, of course, the handed-down words of the Lord had to form the fixed starting point. For the Holy Spirit cannot contradict Himself. If the Spirit has brought us under the leadership of Christ, then what Christ has to say to us now can be only a direct continuation of what He told His Church during His lifetime on earth. If there is to be real leadership then Jesus' present instructions must accord with the commandments of the historical Jesus. This opinion is particularly manifest in the manner in which Paul in 1 Cor. VII takes his stand in the question of marriage. He starts from handed-down words of the Lord which cannot be revoked. Then he adds, as a continuation and a completing commentary to the words of the Lord, that which under the guidance of the Spirit has dawned on him.

As long as we are outside the Christian Church we must necessarily adopt the attitude of a sceptical spectator to the belief of the apostles in guidance by Christ, and say that the apostles and the Church which they founded became the victims of self-deception. What they mistook for inspiration by the living Lord could only have been wild fancies and unconscious wish-complexes. The deterrent example of fanatical movements of every age should moreover warn every student of comparative religion not to place too much value on "voices" and "guidance". But especially if we adopt this sceptical point of view of the spectator does it strike us even more as remarkable that a man like Paul, despite his deplorable experiences with fanatics in his Churches, was not for a moment shaken in his confidence in spiritual guidance by Christ. How

N

much easier his struggle with the fanatics in Corinth would have been if he could have rejected any guidance by the Spirit in advance as a mad error! But all the false imitations of inspiration could not make him doubt the belief that genuine guidance really does exist.

CHAPTER 22

The Possibility and Necessity of the Revelation in Christ to the Present Generation

HOWEVER, THE FACT that the Early Church lived, not merely by the once-and-for-all fact of the Incarnation, but by the continued guidance by Christ, has practical value for us only if we share the fundamental view of the necessity of God's Word, which is common to the Old and the New Testament. The fathers to whom God has spoken (cf. Heb. 1.1) as well as the apostles knew that, although during the whole age before the dissolution of the present form of the world we do get a tremendous impression of almighty God's silent actions and speechless display of power, the interpretation of those actions and immediate access to God are closed to us. To us God lives in an inaccessible light. Consequently we are entirely dependent on the word that only He can speak and without which nature and history remain a book with seven seals.

The coming of Jesus has not made the slightest change in this general condition. The appearance of Christ therefore does not have the meaning, so often ascribed to it, that since then the mystery of the world has been solved and Heaven is open, so that we are no longer dependent on the stages of appeal which lead through the Word, because we have immediate access to the Father. That would be a fanciful attempt to antedate the end of the world, to break through the limitations of the present state of the world and to presume the immediate relation to God which would kill us. Because nothing has been changed in this relationship between God and us, we are entirely dependent, until the end of the present form of the world, on the Son for our communication with the Father. According to 1 Cor. xiv.24-5, it is only at the end that the Son returns the Kingdom to the Father, so that God may be all in all. Till then we need His mediation. Our way to God always leads through Him. Our prayer to the Father is always a prayer in the name of the Son, even if this is not stated in so many words. We can be in God only by remaining in Christ. Only the Spirit which keeps us in contact with the Son witnesses to our spirit that we are God's children (Rom. viii.16). Without the Spirit of the Son the "*Abba*, Father" would be impossible.

It is a dangerous illusion to think that by His coming Jesus has opened to us immediate access to God, that He has in a very simple and optimistic way solved the riddle of the world, that He has shown us that a kind Father is living above the stars. The idea that this concept of the kind Father-God is Christianity has, since the days of the first World War, estranged many of the best men from Christianity. A man who has gone through the second World War has found this superficial belief go to pieces once and for all. For if this were the message of Jesus then we should have to agree with Dwinger: "No, a new God will have to come! For this is sure: the kind old God is dead – he died in the War, like so many other things . . . and this also contains my reply: I have already found this new God! Ah, he is far greater than the God of our good parson . . . for I found him during terrible hours in the camp of Totzkoye, when the army was in retreat – but our parson continues to show us what he learned at the seminary, which has died to us long since, which is lying somewhere in the snow with the men who perished of typhus, among the rats. . . ." In contrast to him it is necessary "to show the new God" who "is a God who maintains himself in the face of the terrible things which happened to mankind during the last ten years . . . ah, he is so much greater, the new God . . ., so much more worthy of us – and of himself".[1]

If Jesus had provided the Church of His disciples for the path of life with this optimistic belief in the god and father of Rationalism, then this god and father would probably not have survived long enough to die in the horrors of the first or the night-raids of the second World War but would have died long before, when the first Christians burned like torches in Nero's gardens and Christian girls were prostituted to the soldiers before their martyrdoms in the circus, without any interference by the heavenly powers to prevent such atrocities. These tor-

[1] Edwin Erich Dwinger, *Wir rufen Deutschland*, Jena 1932, p. 129.

ments however did not for one moment shake the faith of the
first Christians in the Father whom Jesus had shown them.
The terrible martyrdom that came over the Church did not
come as something in the least unexpected, as would have been
the case if they had been brought up to an optimistic belief in
the Father. The Master had prepared them for all this. The
martyr's death was to them merely a "baptism" through which
they entered into the closest relationship with their Master.
They were allowed to die with Christ so as to rise again
together with Him. This shows clearly that the Father to
whom Jesus Himself prayed on the cross and to whom His
disciples prayed in His name right from the beginning was
entirely different from the "old sexagenarian" which Ibsen's
Brand ridicules when he says:

> Old is he haply . . . and, doubtless, white?
> Hairs straggling on a reverend head,
> A beard of ice or silver-thread;
> Kindly, yet stern enough to fright
> A pack of children in the night.
> I will not ask you, if your God
> With fireside slippers you have shod;
> But 'twere a pity, without doubt,
> To leave skull-cap and glasses out.[2]

According to John's Gospel we can grasp the meaning of the
word Father in Jesus' sense only if we look at the one place
where this Father comes forth from the mysteriousness of His
silent action. To the request "Show us the Father" Jesus does
not reply by a calming statement on God's fatherly characteristics. Neither does He make the disciples experience visions
in which God leaves His invisibility to show Himself to the
disciples. He merely says: "He who has seen me has seen the
Father" (Jn. XIV.8-9).

If therefore we seek for a solution of the dark riddle with
which the struggle for power confronts us in the history of the
world with its disorderly medley of wonderful victories and
terrible defeats, then God shows us only the picture of Him
who in the struggle with all the powers of darkness, despised
and ill-treated, on the cross prayed for his murderers and

---

[2] Henrik Ibsen, *Brand*, trans. William Archer, London 1906 (*Collected Works*,
VOL. III), Act I, sc. ii.

finally cried out: "Father into thy hands I commit my spirit."
This picture is put before us with the caption: "He who has
seen me has seen the Father." This is the place from where
alone the eternal light shines in the darkness of time. To Him
we are sent as to the One who alone knows the Father who is
hidden from us. "No one knows the Father except the Son
and anyone to whom the Son chooses to reveal him" (Mt.
xi.27). We therefore do not know the Father. Of His essence
we can grasp only that which the Son reveals to us. All that
in the present state of the world, in which we are unable to
look behind the scenes, we can know about the meaning of it
all, we can know only through Him. As regards the ultimate
question He is our universal Leader. We are dependent on
Him for the question of the future of the world, of guilt and
morality, of power and truth.

The way in which God deals with us men of the time of
Christ is humiliating to our pride, but if we submit to it it leads
us to the goal. God deals with us as one sometimes does with
people who arrive in a completely strange city for the first time.
They want one to give them a complete map of the city with
a clear plan of all the streets and squares, main line and under-
ground railways. With this plan in hand they could make
independent excursions in the city. Instead they are given a
guide and told: you must always follow this man. He will
show you the way, you must not lose sight of him, otherwise
you are like sheep without a shepherd. This method of God is
a great disappointment to our thirst for knowledge and our
urge for a speculative mastery of the world. It makes us painfully conscious of our estrangement from God. But it is no use
whatever protesting against it. For we have no right to interfere with the decisions which God has made for us.

If God instead of a philosophical system or a system of ethics
gives us a personal Leader in whose steps we are to follow, then
this is possible only if this Leader is not merely someone of the
past but someone present who can speak right into our present
situation. He who *a priori* regards this as impossible cannot be
helped by a simple demonstration that the Early Church lived
by faith in the presence of her Lord. For this faith could have
been the product of a primitive mythological way of thinking
which did not yet know the limits set once and for all to com-

munication between persons. To us men of the present day therefore this faith is a possibility only if the essence of the "thou"-relationship as we can now understand it does not exclude a communication between people who have not lived as contemporaries.

In the previous volume of this work[3] it was said in connexion with the discussion of the general structure of the "thou"-relationship that if we regard a real encounter between people who have not lived together as contemporaries as excluded, then this is only because the distinction between "thou"-relationship and "it"-relation has not become clear to us. We conceive of the "thou"-relationship as an objective relation, subject to the laws according to which distances, connexion and separation are possible within the "it"-sphere. We then believe that thou and I can meet and be near to each other only if thy body and my body are near each other in space.

In truth "metaphysical" nearness and distance has nothing to do with bodily nearness and distance. It is possible for you to live in another continent and yet, when I read a letter of yours, to be very close to me and invisibly accompany me in all my movements. On the other hand the body of someone else, e.g. in the narrow space of a tram-car or in the crowds of a large city, can be pressed against mine, and we can even work together in the same office at adjoining desks, and yet be separated as by an ocean, simply have no point of contact whatsoever. The nearness and distance of "I" and "thou" therefore is entirely independent of spatial nearness and distance. It is subject to different laws and is based on different presuppositions.

The nearness between you and me comes into being through the entirely imperceptual and unobjective event which we call understanding. A phenomenon which is entirely within my empirical world, e.g. a line in a letter I have before me, comes to light as a word from you that I immediately understand and affirm with joy. Thereby all that separates us has disappeared in a flash. The spark has flashed across, the electric contact is made, we are together. For, as distinguished from contact between limited objects, the understanding through which in such cases you are brought near to me, as we saw before, is an

[3] *God Transcendent* (pp. 170-1).

encounter between two spaces through which a point of intersection comes into being between two infinities, between your
world and my world. An element of my world distinguishes
itself from its environment as a self-revelation of your being.
This encounter between two spaces, as we saw, is possible only
through an inclusive "space" within which we meet as on a
common level.

This inclusive space, however, which establishes the connexion between your space and my space is something which
we cannot perceive. It is not a space in the sense of perspec-
tively regulated multiplicity as given to me from the one point
from which I see the world. It is beyond all perspective. It is
not like the only space which we know centred around "I".
Otherwise it could not establish communication between the
world as I see it from my perspective centre and the world as
you see it. It could not be the medium in which these two
infinities meet. Therefore the understanding that comes into
being through this unperspective medium is independent of
any spatial relations in which we move. The distance, that is
to say the farness of "thou", which suddenly disappears when
the miracle of understanding takes place, is something that
cannot be expressed in the dimensions of perspective space.
Therefore the removal of that distance, the nearness of "thou",
cannot be compared with any spatial nearness.

But "metaphysical" nearness and distance between you and
me is not only independent of spatial distance but also of distance in time. For the extension of time, as we have shown in
Vol. I,[4] is the form which a happening assumes only after it
has become an objective event. Only as *faits accomplis* do
happenings take their place within the continuum of time and
are inserted there as on a map. Even time therefore, in which
all that happens receives its place, is an objective continuum
that presupposes a point of perspective from which it is regarded. It is the history of the world as it appears before my
eyes when I look back upon it from my point of view, from my
present, and give it a place in the space of my memory.

If therefore a comprehending medium exists that builds the
bridge of understanding between your world and mine, then
this comprehending medium must not only be outside per-

[4] *God Transcendent* (pp. 111-25).

spective space but also outside the extension of time within which events appear from the point of view of a definite ego and a certain present. Therefore the event of understanding is not only independent of spatial distance but also of the distance in time between speaker and hearer.

The encounter between you and me takes place on the level of the present, that is to say on a level which is prior to the extension of time in which accomplished facts are organised. Whether this encounter does or does not take place is entirely independent of how far, within the continuum of time, the events are removed from one another, which as irrevocable results arise from the undecided condition of *becoming*. For this reason leading personalities like Luther and Goethe are understood much better by people living centuries later than by their own contemporaries. There are people who have not been able to acquire an inner relationship to the present but have submerged themselves so deeply in Goethe's world that they experience "hours with Goethe" in which they are not separated from him by any distance. It is in fact quite untrue that we understand a man better, the nearer we are to him in space or time. Under certain circumstances living together in time can even make understanding more difficult, while historical distance can make it easier.

By all this we have, of course, not yet reached the living conversation between "I" and "thou" which, according to II Cor. XII Paul held with the *Kyrios* about the thorn in the flesh. But so much has become evident: the "thou" relationship is not dependent on the objective relations to which we are subject within the space-time continuum. Thereby a new dimension has been opened up to us. From the objective world it is impossible to see what is possible within this other dimension. But we must be prepared for possibilities beyond any objective limitations. For the supra-spective space which establishes the connexion between "I" and "thou" is entirely unfathomable to us because our views are wholly limited to the objective world which we can see and handle. It therefore does not become us to judge what relations are or are not possible within this comprehending medium. Consequently we have no right to declare that a real "thou" relationship with a person who from our point of view belongs to the past is impossible.

What this "thou" relationship to the Leader given to us in the *Kyrios* means to the belief in the reconciliation and the consummation of the world, will be discussed in the third volume of this work, *Jesus der Weltvollender*, Jesus the World's Perfecter.[5]

[5] Karl Heim, *Jesus der Weltvollender*, Hamburg 1952, Engl. trans. *Jesus the World's Perfecter* by D. H. van Daalen, Edinburgh 1959.